ILIAZD

AND

THE ILLUSTRATED BOOK

D1561212

I L I A Z D

AND

THE ILLUSTRATED BOOK

AUDREY ISSELBACHER

ESSAY BY

FRANÇOISE LE GRIS-BERGMANN

THE MUSEUM OF MODERN ART
NEW YORK

Published on the occasion of the exhibition
Iliazd and the Illustrated Book
June 18–August 18, 1987
organized by Audrey Isselbacher, Assistant Curator
Department of Prints and Illustrated Books
The Museum of Modern Art, New York

Frontispiece:
Iliazd setting type at L'Imprimerie Union, Paris, 1962

Copyright © 1987 The Museum of Modern Art, New York

"Iliazd and the Constellation of His Oeuvre"
copyright © 1987 Françoise Le Gris-Bergmann

Mme Le Gris-Bergmann's essay was originally published in French,
in a slightly different version, in *Iliazd, Maître d'oeuvre du livre
moderne,* Montreal: L'Université du Québec à Montréal, 1984.

Translated from the French by Richard Miller

All rights reserved

Library of Congress Catalogue Card Number 87-60361

ISBN 0-87070-396-X

Edited by Maura Walsh
Design and composition by The Sarabande Press, New York
Production by Susan Schoenfeld
Printed by Eastern Press, New Haven
Bound by Mueller Trade Bindery, Middletown, Connecticut

The Museum of Modern Art
11 West 53 Street
New York, New York 10019

Distributed outside the United States and Canada by Thames and
Hudson Ltd., London

Printed in the United States of America

CONTENTS

ACKNOWLEDGMENTS

This exhibition and catalogue would not have been possible without the invaluable participation of several individuals and institutions to whom I am extremely grateful. First and foremost is Hélène Iliazd, who generously shared with me her extensive archive and unequaled expertise on her late husband's life and work, providing both crucial loans of books and their preparatory material as well as rare documentary photographs for the catalogue. Her infinite patience and devotion to this project have made our collaboration a truly enriching experience. Sincere thanks are also due Riva Castleman, the Museum's Deputy Director for Curatorial Affairs and Director of the Department of Prints and Illustrated Books, who initiated the concept of an exhibition of Iliazd's books in 1977. Her indispensable advice and ongoing encouragement have been essential elements in the project's realization.

Raymond J. Learsy, a keen admirer and collector of Iliazd's publications, has similarly played a critical role by generously lending his own copies of several books. I am indebted as well to Marie Bertin, Paris; the Bibliothèque Nationale, Paris; and The New York Public Library for lending to the exhibition. Françoise Le Gris-Bergmann, Professor of Art History at L'Université du Québec à Montréal, who organized an exhibition of Iliazd's work for that institution in 1984, very kindly allowed us to reprint her illuminating essay in a somewhat reduced form. Other individuals who played key roles in the course of my research are Louis Barnier, Director of L'Imprimerie Union, Paris; Antoine Coron, Curator at La Réserve des Imprimés, Bibliothèque Nationale, Paris; Elizabeth Phillips, New York; Robert Rainwater, Assistant Director for Art, Prints, and Photographs and Curator, Spencer Collection, The New York Public Library; and Roberta Wadell, Curator of Prints, also of The New York Public Library.

I wish to thank the members of the staff of the Museum who have expertly assisted in the preparation of the exhibition and of this catalogue: Richard L. Palmer, Coordinator of Exhibitions; Betsy Jablow, Associate Coordinator of Exhibitions; Jerry Neuner, Production Manager, Exhibition Program; Janet Hawkins, Assistant Registrar; Richard L. Tooke, Supervisor of Rights and Reproductions; and Tim McDonough, Publications Production Manager. I was extremely fortunate to have the knowledgeable assistance of Kathleen Slavin, Curatorial Assistant in the Department of Prints and Illustrated Books, who enthusiastically participated in all aspects of this project. My admiration and gratitude are due Maura Walsh, Assistant Editor, who thoughtfully edited this catalogue, Joe Marc Freedman of The Sarabande Press, who sensitively executed its design, and Susan Schoenfeld, Assistant Production Manager, who capably oversaw the essential details of its production.

Support for the exhibition and catalogue has been provided through the generosity of Walter Bareiss, Loriano Bertini, Raymond J. Learsy, the late Arthur Stanton, Mrs. Alfred R. Stern, The Associates of the Department of Prints and Illustrated Books, the Cosmopolitan Arts Foundation, and an anonymous donor. To these friends of the illustrated book I owe my deepest appreciation.

A. I.

I L I A Z D

AND

THE ILLUSTRATED BOOK

PIROSMANACHVILI

ILIAZD AND THE TRADITION OF THE "LIVRE DE PEINTRE"

Audrey Isselbacher

Fig. 1. Iliazd. Cover for *Pirosmanachvili 1914* by Iliazd. Paris, Le Degré Quarante et Un, 1972. Typographical composition, 12½ × 9½″ (31.8 × 24.2 cm). The Museum of Modern Art, New York. Mrs. Stanley Resor Fund (by exchange)

Fig. 2. Pablo Picasso. Frontispiece for *Pirosmanachvili 1914* by Iliazd. Paris, Le Degré Quarante et Un, 1972. Drypoint, 12⅛ × 7¼″ (30.8 × 18.4 cm). The Museum of Modern Art, New York. Mrs. Stanley Resor Fund (by exchange)

A cloth-covered box with a strange symbol stamped on its side provides no clue to the magic of its contents. The removal of this slipcase reveals a crude jacket of rough butcher's paper bearing the confusing title *Pirosmanachvili*, which yields in turn an unbound book housed in parchment. Withdrawn from these elaborate coverings, numerous inner folders of blank, creamy stock lead gradually to the heart of the book, an assortment of distinctly narrower folios of ancient japan paper. An embossed rectangle on the first narrow leaf signals an end to the smooth emptiness and raises the possibility of a printed image on the other side. A turn of the page reveals Picasso's small-scale yet monumental frontispiece, a portrait of the Georgian naïve painter Niko Pirosmanachvili (1862–1918). The formal title page it faces, printed in the boldly unadorned typeface found on the book's cover, makes certain information clear: author, Iliazd; title, *Pirosmanachvili 1914;* artist, Picasso; medium, drypoint; and publisher, The 41st Degree. But by now the reader knows not to expect the conventional sequence of text. No less than six blank pages precede an untitled preface, soberly laid out without punctuation in variably spaced letters of the stark Gill typeface. Two additional blank pages lead finally to Iliazd's essay on the artist, set in an equally ascetic fashion and mysteriously concealed on the inner leaves of eight numbered folios. His text ends as abruptly as it began, and a colophon describing edition size, paper type, printer, and other details of publication serves as the last printed element of the volume. There follows a sequence of blank pages identical to that which opened the book, ensuring a gentle transition back to the ordinariness of the outside world.

To describe *Pirosmanachvili 1914* (published 1972; figs. 1 and 2) as a small book with a short text by Iliazd, a frontispiece by Picasso, and quantities of blank pages would be an accurate but inadequate summation. It would give no indication of the appeal of Iliazd's inventive design, which resonates with contextual significance. Just as early in his life Iliazd discovered the art of the unknown Pirosmanachvili, the reader, too, must decipher the volume's intricately paced contents. Moreover, it is no exaggeration to say that Iliazd buried his homage to the dead artist in a profusion of protective paper shrouds. Even the oblong format and austere typographical layout are suggestive, echoing as they do the shape of a tombstone and the lettering of an epitaph. Finally, the process of reading the text, intentionally prolonged by so many unexpected pauses, is designed to heighten awareness of the endless passage of time.

The little-known Iliazd, a dynamic figure in the modern movement, designed and produced a handful of the most innovative illustrated books of this century. Born Ilia Zdanevitch in 1894 in Tiflis, Georgia, he emigrated to Paris in 1921. His early espousal of Marinetti's Futurist theories and intense involvement with Russian avant-garde poetry contributed significantly to the formation of his unique approach to the *livre de peintre*, or "painter's book." The product of an era in which all things were thought possible, Iliazd conceived of the illustrated book as a means to "revise human values," and he successfully imposed this vision on such formidable collaborators as Jean Arp, Max Ernst, Alberto Giacometti, Henri Matisse, Joan Miró, Pablo Picasso, and Jacques Villon. Poet, novelist, playwright, archeologist, and student of Byzantine architecture, Iliazd brought a wide-ranging intellectual curiosity to his work as a publisher, and he often initiated unlikely collaborations between artists and authors. Through his inventive handling of typography and his imaginative folding and arrangement of folios, Iliazd created enlightening juxtapositions of text and image. In 1940, under the imprint The 41st Degree (a cryptic reference to the latitude of Tiflis, the alcoholic content of brandy, and the Celsius measure of a delirium-producing fever), Iliazd published his first *de luxe* book, *Afat* (plate 10), a suite of his own sonnets embellished with six engravings by Picasso. From that time until his death in 1975, he continued to produce books of exceptional quality with some of the most important painters and sculptors of the twentieth century. Because these publications fit into the classic French tradition of the *livre de peintre*, it is illuminating to consider them within that context.

The phenomenon of the modern *livre de peintre* began in the nineteenth century, as painters and not merely professional engravers began to execute original prints to complement literary works. During the 1880s, the introduction of photographic techniques caused a decline in the quality of illustrated books, resulting in disjointed volumes with photomechanical reproductions by minor artists. William Morris in England and Edouard Pelletan in France were among the first publishers to respond to this decline, focusing their efforts on the typographical setting of the text. During the 1890s, artists and authors became increasingly sensitive to the complexities of attaining an inspired harmony of text and image. Maurice Denis was one of the first modern painters to take up this challenge, with his boldly simple illustrations and asymmetrically designed pages for a 1911 edition of Paul Verlaine's *Sagesse*. One of the first authors to supervise the printing of his own text, Stéphane Mallarmé sought to express poetic cadence through an irregular typographical format in an unrealized edition of *Un Coup de dés jamais n'abolira le hasard* with lithographs by Odilon Redon. These two critical projects shared a common publisher, Ambroise Vollard, with whom the history of the twentieth-century *livre de peintre* begins.

Ambroise Vollard arrived in Paris from the Indian Ocean island of La Réunion in 1890 to study law, but pursued instead his love for art, establishing the gallery that in 1895 would mount the first exhibition of Cézanne's paintings. Vollard's subsequent issuing of fine albums of original prints by modern painters ultimately nurtured his true passion, illustrated books, and in 1900 a daring edition of Paul Verlaine's *Parallèlement* (fig. 3) marked Vollard's entry into this specialized art form. Bonnard's fluidly drawn lithographs for *Parallèlement*, unbound by conventional restrictions segregating text from image, spill over into margins and areas normally reserved for printed words, creating a brilliant fusion of picture and verse. The venturesome spirit of this artist's approach to book illustration appropriately matched the author's risqué text, but the publisher must be credited with having accepted and supported Bonnard's inspired solution. For this *livre de peintre*, Vollard succumbed to the allure of a beautiful typeface first used in sixteenth-century France, Garamond, "that magnificent type engraved by order of François I, the italics of which seemed to me expressly designed to print the work of a poet,"[1] demonstrating both his disdain for modern type and his concern for the text's proper appearance. In twenty-seven subsequent volumes completed between 1900 and 1939, the year of his death, Vollard commonly allowed artists to illustrate works of their choosing, including fiction and poetry by established French masters and classical Roman or Greek literature. Although he once said "I am the architect of my books,"[2] Vollard gave his artists free rein in their interpretation of a given text, focusing his own participation on the maintenance of the highest technical and material standards. His monumental conception of the *livre de peintre* is reflected in the scale of the books themselves, many of which comprise more than one hundred illustrations and were printed in editions of as many as 250 copies. Neither time nor expense were spared as Vollard went on to produce or initiate the production of some of the most sumptuous illustrated books of this century, by artists such as Marc Chagall, Pablo Picasso, and Georges Rouault.

Whereas Vollard generally oriented his publications toward their pictorial component, Daniel-Henry Kahnweiler exercised a more balanced control over author and artist. In 1907, the twenty-two-year-old native German opened a gallery in Paris to show the work of the Cubists and Fauves, and his desire to publish illustrated books sprang from the communal spirit of poets and painters he met in their Bâteau-Lavoir studios. Kahnweiler's first publication, Guillaume Apollinaire's *L'Enchan-*

Fig. 3. Pierre Bonnard. *Parallèlement* by Paul Verlaine. Paris, Ambroise Vollard, 1900. Lithograph, printed in color, 11⅝ × 9½" (29.5 × 24.1 cm). The Museum of Modern Art, New York. The Louis E. Stern Collection

Fig. 4. André Derain. *L'Enchanteur pourrissant* by Guillaume Apollinaire. Paris, Henry Kahnweiler, 1909. Woodcut, 10⅛ × 8" (25.7 × 20.3 cm). The Museum of Modern Art, New York. The Louis E. Stern Collection

Fig. 5. Henri Matisse. *Poésies de Stéphane Mallarmé*. Lausanne, Albert Skira & Cie., 1932. Etching, 13 × 10" (33 × 25.4 cm). The Museum of Modern Art, New York. The Louis E. Stern Collection

teur pourrissant with woodcuts by André Derain (published 1909; fig. 4), was a milestone, being the first text by Apollinaire released in book form and the first volume containing original illustrations by Derain. Derain's "neoprimitive" woodcuts, more ornamental than literal, were as avant-garde as Apollinaire's mystical text, and the overall simplicity of this modestly sized book stands in sharp contrast to the abundant excesses of Vollard's elegant editions. Kahnweiler's ongoing involvement with contemporary painters and poets enabled him to issue many previously unpublished texts and illustrations by authors and artists such as Max Jacob, André Malraux, Antonin Artaud, Pablo Picasso, Juan Gris, and André Masson. In the thirty-six illustrated books issued by Kahnweiler over his almost fifty-year career (1920–69), the meaningful consolidation of text and image remained his primary concern, an ideal facilitated by the publisher's intelligent open-mindedness and intuitive ability to juggle the wishes of both artist and author. Primarily committed to presenting new and difficult works, Kahnweiler maintained a straightforward approach in his book designs. Both edition size and format remained modest: the typical edition size was one hundred, and the number of illustrations was often less than ten. While Kahnweiler, like Vollard, was exacting regarding technical and material matters, his subtle, intellectual approach produced landmark syntheses of the literary and visual arts in which neither component overshadowed the other.

In contrast to Kahnweiler's restrained volumes stand the lavishly decorated editions of Albert Skira, whose first *livres de peintres*—Ovid's *Metamorphoses* with etchings by Picasso (published 1931) and *Poésies de Stéphane Mallarmé* with etchings by Matisse (published 1932; fig. 5)—brought the Swiss publisher immediate recognition as an insightful impresario. Skira began publishing in Lausanne in 1928 with a lofty ambition: to have Picasso illustrate his first book. It was not until two years later that the master finally kept his promise to execute original prints for a *livre de peintre*, agreeing to work on Ovid's *Metamorphoses*. It was Skira who indicated the most appropriate passages to illustrate, and the resulting images, fruits of Picasso's classical linear phase, prove the wisdom of his choices. With similar perception, Skira cleverly appreciated that the poetry of the etched line of Matisse, who had never before attempted book illustration, would be a perfect counterpoint to Mallarmé's verse. The graceful elegance of Skira's *Poésies* typifies his unerring insistence on absolute harmony between text and image. To achieve this goal, he designed his books in a modern yet traditional style, and his concern for typographical integrity precluded unnecessary distractions from the dialogue between word and picture. After such fruitful collaborations with Picasso and Matisse, Skira went on to produce a total of only seven *livres de peintres*, commissioning as illustrators, predominantly of classical texts, the artists Salvador Dali, André Derain, André Beaudin, and André Masson. He upheld perfectionist standards in the production of these exquisite volumes, forming long-term relationships with trusted printers, providing precise printing instructions, and allowing sufficient time for the book-making process. Skira, like Vollard, printed all his books in large editions with numerous illustrations. The pressing monetary and technical demands inherent in Skira's impeccable concept of the *livre de peintre* forced him to abandon this exacting pursuit after 1949. In the years that followed, Skira pioneered the publication of fine-quality art books, but his inspirational vision of the artist-illustrated book must be considered an equally profound contribution.

It was the young Tériade who suggested to Skira that pivotal collaboration with Matisse. Born Efstratios Eleftheriades in Lesbos, Tériade arrived in Paris in 1915 to study law. He quickly became involved in art, initially through his work on the first issues of Skira's review *Cahiers d'Art* and later in the early 1930s as director of Skira's famous Surrealist publication, *Minotaure*. This exposure to the liberated Dada and Surrealist literary milieu brought Tériade in close contact with such key figures as André Breton, Paul Eluard, and Tristan Tzara, and left its mark on his vision of the *livre de peintre* as a free-flowing, organic entity. Tériade's distinct contribution to the twentieth-century illustrated book, the introduction of handwritten texts, was an indirect result of this liberated approach. His gift of friendly persuasion elicited highly personal responses from artists, and for a 1948 edition of *Le Chant des morts* by Pierre Reverdy (fig. 6), Picasso forcefully integrated his lithographic images directly into the poet's calligraphy. Allowing Picasso to unselfconsciously interfere with his collaborator's hand-written words typified Tériade's laissez-faire policy, under which, more often than not, the artist himself engineered a book's overall design. Artists were likewise free to propose texts to illustrate, and the roster of authors published by Tériade affirms the diversity of their choices, which ranged from contemporary artists' writings to the literature of classical Greece. The freedom Tériade accorded his artists is also reflected in their varying interpretations of the role of illustrator. Matisse, for example, executed the compositions for *Jazz* (published 1947) before the existence of his accompanying text. Tériade released twenty-six books in twenty-eight years (1943–71), working primarily with Marc Chagall, Marcel Gromaire, Henri Laurens, Fernand Léger, Henri Matisse, and Joan Miró. His *livres de peintres* were always impressive undertakings, generally printed in editions of over two hundred and usually containing more than thirty illustrations. If not as exclusively devoted to the promotion of progressive painters and poets as Kahnweiler, Tériade made the invaluable contribution of encouraging artists to uninhibitedly explore the illustrated book's unique potential for visual drama.

These four major figures in the history of the twentieth-century *livre de peintre* held in common certain attributes that were fundamental to the success of their publications. Most important, each possessed the compelling vision and guiding presence from which the pervading unity of any masterful edition derives. In addition, keen aesthetic judgment enabled them to forge auspicious

Fig. 6. Pablo Picasso. *Le Chant des morts* by Pierre Reverdy. Paris, Tériade Editeur, 1948. Lithograph, printed in color, 16½ × 12⅝" (42 × 32 cm). The Museum of Modern Art, New York. The Louis E. Stern Collection

unions between artists and authors and to produce books reflective of these inspired collaborations. The power of persuasion was likewise an essential talent, for all of these publishers inevitably needed to convince hesitant artists and authors of the merit of their collaborations. The imagination and persistence to foresee and ultimately attain the rewards of an extremely time-consuming and expensive undertaking were similarly indispensable traits. Finally, although their unwillingness to compromise their high technical standards ensured the execution of quality work, the right amount of flexibility regarding creative decisions fostered fruitful cooperative efforts.

A review of the twenty extraordinary *livres de peintres* designed and published by Iliazd between 1940 and 1974 clearly confirms that he possessed all of these qualities except one, flexibility, the marked absence of which provides the key to understanding his unique contribution to the illustrated book: he absolutely refused to relinquish control over either the form or content of his publications. Iliazd's publishing approach, deeply influenced by the Russian avant-garde's use of printed material to relay activist messages, was idealistic and noncommercial.

> I do not publish editions for monetary gain. I struggle. I have always struggled for an idea, and if I published such and such an author, it is always to bring attention to an unknown, and not only to reestablish him, but also to turn the tide of ideas toward him, to revise, once again, human values.[3]

Iliazd's very first *de luxe* book, *Afat*, whose title derives from an Arabic word meaning unhappiness or the beauty who inspires unhappy love, offers practical evidence of this. Its colophon proudly states that the copperplates for Picasso's engravings were not steel-faced (electroplated for added strength so that a larger edition could be printed). This adherence to a purist concept of printing resulted in visually rich impressions but held the edition size of *Afat* to sixty-four copies, a meager yield when compared with the standard one- or two-hundred-copy editions of *livres de peintres* published by his colleagues.

Iliazd's particular devotion to undiscovered authors and artists extended beyond the release of his own writings and surpassed boundaries of both time and place. He published *Poésie de mots inconnus* (plates 12–16), an anthology of original Futurist and Dada texts predominantly from the 1920s, in Paris in 1949. Iliazd's broad personal interests in architecture, ballet, astronomy, and the early explorers inspired several of his editions, and the eclecticism of his taste is further evidenced in the many unlikely unions he forged between authors and artists. A case in point is his 1974 edition of Adrian de Monluc's *Le Courtisan grotesque* (plates 38 and 39), a sardonic seventeenth-century tale of an unattractive courtier, which is whimsically illustrated by Miró's colorful etchings.

That Iliazd exerted total control over the selection of the text is unquestioned. Picasso, in his first commissions for Iliazd—*Afat* and *Pismo* ("The Letter"; plate 11)—was unable even to read Iliazd's Russian poems, and was forced to rely on the poet/publisher's verbal conveyance of their narrative content to formulate his imagery. This strict supervision of the literary aspect of his *livres de peintres* is irrefutably tied to Iliazd's early linguistic experimentation. The *zaum* or "transrational" group of Russian avant-garde poets advocated the redefinition of language based purely on words' sounds, and Iliazd was one of this movement's most creative participants. Such intense investigations into the very core of verbal communication never left Iliazd's consciousness, and he consequently had a more vested interest in a book's text than most other *livre de peintre* publishers. Of the twenty *de luxe* editions issued by The 41st Degree, eight are of Iliazd's own writings, while the remaining twelve are of works by friends or authors from earlier centuries that appealed to his literary sensibility.

Iliazd's intense involvement with the *zaum* movement also encompassed typographical experimentation, culminating in the 1923 volume *lidantYU fAram* ("Ledentu as Beacon"; plates 7 and 8), in which an astonishing variety of typefaces, type sizes, and arrangements of characters explodes across the page. This basic preoccupation with the "look" of a text never diminished, and Iliazd himself designed the typography for all of his subsequent publications. His layouts were always informed by his personal interpretation of a given text, a concern for complementing the narrative that extended to his selection of artists as well. Regarding the choice of Michel Guino to illustrate the 1965 publication *Un Soupçon* (plate 33), a fifteen-line minimalist poem by Paul Eluard, Iliazd said, "If I approached the sculptor Michel Guino, it is because I thought that his style would go well with a work in which the word 'légère' is repeated so many times."[4] Regarding his typographical concept for the 1952 edition *La Maigre* (plates 17 and 18), in which he introduced the variable spacing and the neutral Gill font he used exclusively thereafter, Iliazd wrote:

> It is in this book that I introduced for the first time the exclusive use of variable spacing between letters in order to balance and lighten the lines. This invention demonstrated the error committed by Renaissance artists in their quest for proportions of rounded letters as they studied each letter separately instead of envisioning the [typographical] whole.[5]

Iliazd's organization of the text on a given page was ingeniously calculated. In *Chevaux de minuit* (fig. 7), which was published in 1956, the staccato layout of Roch Grey's epic poem gallops, trots, and leaps in the company of Picasso's engraved horses. In *Un Soupçon*, a musical scale–like design of type playfully mimics the nuances of Paul Eluard's melodic poem. In *Hommage à Roger Lacourière* (published 1968; plates 35–37), the graduated configuration of Iliazd's text is symbolic, subliminally evocative of the steep stairway to Sacré Coeur that led to Roger Lacourière's printing studio in

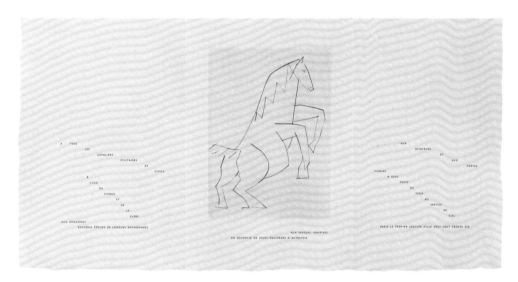

Fig. 7. Pablo Picasso. *Chevaux de minuit* by Roch Grey. Cannes and Paris, Aux bons soins du Degré Quarante et Un, 1956. Drypoint and engraving; unfolded folio: 12⅛ × 24³⁄₁₆″ (30.8 × 61.4 cm). The Museum of Modern Art, New York. The Louis E. Stern Collection

Montmartre. While most of his colleagues aimed for a conceptual correspondence between typography and text and searched for rare and exquisite typefaces, Iliazd, through his "painterly" manipulation of the most banal type, created lively compositions of lines, angles, and curves.

Iliazd's meticulous attention to typographical arrangement was paralleled by his concern for the "architecture" of the book as a whole. His concept of striking a harmonious balance between word and image was so uncompromising that he himself decided the precise number, format, and placement of the illustrations, often providing artists with copperplates or woodblocks already cut to size. These rigorous calculations were based on the position of images within the overall configuration of folios and created animated sequences of typographical and/or illustrative pages that often formed patterns. *La Maigre* is constructed in a classic ABCBCBCBA scheme, comprised of alternating leaves of three distinct page layouts.[6] An additional architectural element is the folding of the individual folios. In *Pismo*, published in 1948, sheets are irregularly folded and conjoined to create a puzzlelike division of pages into thirds in a clever allusion to the narrative's trio: the painter Picasso, the poet Iliazd, and the muse Olga Djordjadzé (the Russian compatriot to whom Iliazd addressed this poetic letter).[7]

Before a sheet could be printed, folded, and inserted into the proper place, its texture, color, and receptivity to ink were carefully determined by Iliazd. Preferring the satiny surfaces of china and japan papers so luxuriously responsive to the critical combination of pressure, matrix, and ink, Iliazd searched for the perfect stock as though he were hunting for treasure. For *Sillage intangible* (published 1958; plate 27), a poetic memorial to the deceased Eluard, he chose "the most beautiful japan paper one could find in Paris, that which the publisher Pelletan acquired in 1906 from Bing, exporter of items from China and Japan."[8] A remarkable bound copy of *Le Frère mendiant, o Libro del conocimiento* (published 1959; plates 23–26), a tale of the fourteenth-century voyages of an anonymous Franciscan monk, contains triplicate proofs of each of Picasso's drypoints printed on china, imperial japan, and ancient japan papers, the varying opacities of which produce enchanting superimpositions. Deciphering these pictorial minglings becomes an adventure uncannily suited to a narrative about geographic exploration.

Iliazd's concern for a book's architecture was combined with a marked inclination toward theatricality, a tendency born of his early activity in the Russian literary avant-garde. Between 1916 and 1923, he wrote the *Aslaablitchia* ("Dunkeyness") cycle of five *dras* (plates 2, 4–8), one-act plays based on a form of Ukrainian puppet theater, and this experience enhanced his profound understanding of how to create an atmosphere of drama. This perception is readily apparent in the elaborate containers Iliazd fashioned for his *livres de peintres*, always comprising numerous layers of covers, folders, and envelopes inserted together, unbound, into a single slipcase. At times, the dramatic quality of a volume's architecture is contextually relevant, as in the narrow vertical format of *La Maigre*, a biting satire on the vanity of an excruciatingly thin woman written by Adrian de Monluc in 1630. Its stiff parchment cover is impossible to open—one must remove the leaves to read them—and even the fibrous folder around the parchment is rough and dry to the touch, like the brittle and rigid character so vividly described by Monluc.

In spite of the many conceptual and material considerations implicit in Iliazd's innovative approach to book publishing and design, his hallmark remains the endowment of each publication with a predominant sense of clarity and purpose. Brutally plain by the standards of a Vollard edition, devoid of seductively decorative initials, chapter headings, or separate suites of illustrations, Iliazd's *livres de peintres* nevertheless possess a monumental quality in which the harmonious coexistence of text and image prevails. Through his unique synthesis of two opposite traditions, the Russian utilitarian booklet and the *de luxe* French illustrated book, Iliazd championed esoteric yet humanistic causes in a sumptuous format. Paradoxically, his own avoidance of celebrity consigned the poet/publisher to the same realm of obscurity from which he drew material for his books: Iliazd is not well known outside the specialized world of the bibliophile. If he truly believed, as he wrote in the afterword of *La Maigre*, that "to fall into oblivion is the poet's best fate," Iliazd has surely fulfilled his preferred destiny. In spite of the poet's wish, however, the publisher's impulse to conceive lasting monuments to literature and art has left behind a brilliant and enduring legacy.

Notes

1. Quoted in W. J. Strachan, *The Artist and the Book in France* (New York: George Wittenborn, 1969), pp. 38–39.

2. Quoted in Una Johnson, *Ambroise Vollard, Editeur* (New York: The Museum of Modern Art, 1977), p. 29.

3. Iliazd to Joan Miró, letter of 4 May 1961. Quoted in "Correspondance Iliazd–Miró, A propos du 'Courtisan grotesque,'" in *Iliazd, Maître d'oeuvre du livre moderne*, exhibition catalogue, L'Université du Québec à Montréal, 1984, p. 118.

4. Quoted in Annick Lionel-Marie, "Iliazd, Facettes d'une vie," in *Iliazd*, exhibition catalogue, Centre Georges Pompidou, Musée National d'Art Moderne, Paris, 1978, p. 81.

5. Ibid., p. 68.

6. See Louis Barnier, "Iliazd, notre compagnon . . ." in *Iliazd*, pp. 23–32.

7. See Sebastian Goeppert, Herma Goeppert-Frank, and Patrick Cramer, *Pablo Picasso, The Illustrated Books: Catalogue Raisonné* (Geneva: Patrick Cramer, Publisher, 1983), p. 132.

8. Quoted in François Chapon, "Catalogue," in *La Rencontre Iliazd–Picasso, Hommage à Iliazd*, exhibition catalogue, Musée d'Art Moderne de la Ville de Paris, 1976, *Sillage intangible* entry.

ILIAZD AND THE CONSTELLATION OF HIS OEUVRE

Françoise Le Gris-Bergmann

Any consideration of Iliazd's contribution to the modern illustrated book must include, first, some examination of his particular concept of the publisher's *métier*. In the case of Iliazd, his work as a publisher was clearly reinforced by his work as a writer and, above all, a poet. And of course his youthful years of apprenticeship in the Caucasus as a typographer/printer were also influential. In Iliazd's career these two basic experiences, as well as his passion for modern art, which he ardently defended from his earliest days in Russian avant-garde circles, formed the basis for a view of the book as both an object and a receptacle, as a site as well as a stage, as an emanation of the Word as well as of a kind of choreographic imaging. The site also of ruptures, in Iliazd's work the book as object paradoxically takes on a kind of ritualistic quality. One example of this is Iliazd's use of exclusively capital letters, which in the language of his native Georgia distinguishes ecclesiastic from profane or military writings. Thus Iliazd's unique view of the publishing *métier* must be understood in light of his unique formative context, one that was, of necessity, to guide his later achievements.

Second, we must attempt to deal with Iliazd's work as a whole, one not lacking internal variation and modulation, but a whole that nevertheless reveals a certain continuity. Indeed, we might describe the development of his oeuvre as being circular, reminiscent of the movements of stars and planets in a particular constellation. Iliazd forms the center of this constellation, which is made up of many and diverse names: Niko Pirosmanachvili, Adrian de Monluc, Mikhail Ledentu, Marie-Laure de Noailles, Roch Grey, Kiril Zdanevitch, Ernst Wilhelm Tempel, and many more. His places are equally varied: Tiflis, Moscow, St. Petersburg, Paris, Toulouse, the African coast, etc. And his oeuvre encompasses many mediums, book-making, first, but also theater, dance, and writing. The contours of a body of work that is polymorphous, eclectic, difficult to take in at a glance, but at the same time strikingly cohesive—that is what we shall attempt to evoke here.

THE FOUNDATIONS OF AN OEUVRE

From Tiflis to Paris's rue Mazarine, although time and events have brought great changes to both, we can discern a certain continuity between the major concerns of Iliazd's youth and his mature work. We know that Iliazd, then known as Ilia Zdanevitch, arrived in St. Petersburg in September of 1911 "already a confirmed Futurist,"[1] and that he immediately began to take part in the activities of the artistic avant-garde: "Through his

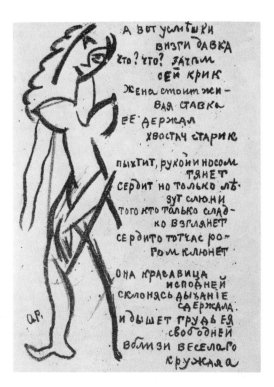

Fig. 1. Olga Rozanova. *The Game in Hell* by Alexei Kruchenykh and Victor Khlebnikov. St. Petersburg, Svet, 1913–14. Lithograph, 7 1/16 × 5" (17.9 × 12.7 cm). The Museum of Modern Art, New York. Gift of Donald Karshan, in honor of the Museum's 50th Anniversary

brother Kiril, he met the painters Victor Barthe and Mikhail Ledentu, who introduced him into avant-garde circles. He immediately took a stand against the Symbolists' attachment to the past and engaged in fervent propaganda for Futurism."[2] His familiarity with the small illustrated books published in St. Petersburg during the "flamboyant period of Russian Futurism" (Iliazd's phrase) was undoubtedly crucial. Indeed, this series of hand-printed works is one of the more innovative and remarkable experiments of the Russian avant-garde.[3] Iliazd's close connection with these unique publications, long before he (with the poets Alexei Kruchenykh and Igor Terentiev) founded his own press, The 41st Degree, is confirmed by his personal library, which contained some of the more significant of these works.

Through these publications (which we will call Futurist for the sake of simplicity) Iliazd discovered, among other things, the close relationship between poetry and "picturality" (fig. 1). Of course, all movements calling for artistic autonomy are committed, in poetry as well as in painting, to achieving a certain materialism in artistic conception, from "the word as such" and "the letter as such" (Victor Khlebnikov, Kruchenykh),[4] to form and color as such (Malevitch), to the "culture of materials" (Tatlin). However, the site furnished by the book afforded artists the opportunity to experiment with the modernist dimensions inherent in a synthesis of poetry/painting, text/figure, system of viewing/system of creating. Like theater, the book is an inherently synthetic form. Thus the realization of new modes of expression through the book was intensified when it came to incorporating the two dimensions inherent in written language: a "thrust" toward the graphic and the use of the voice, the phoneticization of the sign.

In fact, here we must consider two kinds of principles. First, there is Futurist poetry's disintegration of the word in its progress toward *zaum*, toward a purely phonetic

poetry, toward the deconstruction of the word's verbal mass so as to conserve—or at least favor—its sonority (its phonemes). Such poetry, in the act of inscribing, transcribing, itself, deconstructs its written shape, destroys the conventions of order and form, and forces its written shape into new spatial configurations. Such a self-assertive graphic substance can no longer camouflage itself behind its transparency to the meaning of its words, but must become expressive in and of itself, must ally itself with the artist's drawing, his "graphism." The book then becomes the site where the two graphic forms meet, one with a sonoral referentiality, the other endowed first with a pictorial existence (colors, features, shapes, lines). Both forms come together in the book in a new synthesis, at once and indissociably both picture and text.

All such innovative experiments can in a way be viewed as signs of an adherence to "Futurism," a "magic" word signifying the new man in a new world.[5] However, that convenient label covers a range of different, if not divergent, allegiances and positions. The underlying factor common to all these movements and the achievements made in their names was a widespread desire to break the bonds of Symbolism confining artistic production in the early twentieth century, and to destroy the outmoded formulas of the World of Art group. The close relationship of painting and poetry was likewise a fundamental element in these Russian avant-garde groups. Indeed, bolstered by the innovative experiments carried out in both poetry and painting in the early years of this century (c. 1908–09), artists joined efforts to achieve a completely synthetic form of expression, the illustrated book, which forged a "sacred alliance" between painters and poets. A felicitous and reciprocal emancipation followed in the artistic languages of both painting and poetry, each form of expression having a dynamic effect upon the other.

Fig. 2. Photograph of Iliazd (right), Mikhail Larionov, and Natalia Gontcharova with painted faces, November 8, 1913, published with their manifesto "Why We Paint Our Faces" in the Moscow journal *Argus*, December 1913

Iliazd had been involved in this alliance between poets and painters even before the founding of The 41st Degree (c. 1916–17). We know that he had been in Larionov's circle, taking an active part in the formulation of the theories associated with Larionov (and Gontcharova): "neoprimitivism," Rayonism, and *vsechestvo*, or "everythingism." And we know that he took part in group actions and public statements in support of these theories, such as the "Why We Paint Our Faces" demonstration and article (fig. 2).

Apart from the preponderant role Iliazd played in the actual formulation of Larionov's Rayonism,[6] the "poet Zdanevitch" (Iliazd) stated, in a 1913 "declaration on Futurism":

Futurism exists neither in the Jack of Diamonds nor in the Union of Youth; Gontcharova and Larionov alone have attained it. We must free ourselves from dependence on the exterior world. In Rayonism, painting is free . . . Impressionism gave color, Cubism the third dimension, Futurism found the style of movement and Rayonism has synthesized them all.[7]

This statement is important because Iliazd later maintained that he had been the first "Rayonist poet." At the end of his 1913 book *Mikhail Larionov/Natalia Gontcharova* (plate 1) Iliazd announced the forthcoming publication of a collection of "Rayonist" poetry. This would appear to be the first evidence of any poetic activity on Iliazd's part.[8] Although in later years Iliazd always denied having written any poetry during this period, it is very probable that in fact he did (most likely under the pseudonym Lotov); he always enjoyed playing games of this sort, and mentioned the name of the mysterious and obscure Lotov on several occasions later in his life. We can assume that there must have been some Rayonist poems on the basis of Iliazd's early essential knowledge of the work involved in publishing such

poetry (from the writing stage to the page-layout stage). Before there was any question of *zaum* or "transmental" poetry ("poetry of the beyond"), the publication of this earlier poetry served as a laboratory for experiments that contributed significantly to the development of *zaum* and other modernist trends in Russian literature.

Upon his return to Tiflis in the Caucasus in 1917, Iliazd broadened the scope of his publishing experiments.

At the end of 1917 we transported . . . our publications into the mountains of the Caucasus, where the conditions for pursuing our work were better. Accompanied by two of the best contemporary Russian poets, A. Kruchenykh and I. Terentiev, I founded The 41st Degree company, and for two years we had two magazines in which we could publish our experiments and our works. The 41st Degree lasted for almost 20 issues, while in the North poetry of all kinds was degenerating.[9]

It was in this context that Iliazd published four of the five pieces he referred to as *dras* ("dra(ma)s"), of the *Aslaablitchia* ("Dunkeyness") cycle,[10] namely, *Yanko krul' albanskai* ("Yanko, King of Albania"; plate 2), *Ostraf paskhi* ("Easter Eyeland"; plate 4), *Asel naprakat* ("Dunkey for Rent"; plate 5), and *zgA YAkaby* ("As if Zga"; plate 6). While developing his *zaum* language in a particularly rich and rigorous way, Iliazd also experimented, with admirable results, with the typographical layout of his work. This latter activity yielded some of the most convincing and advanced examples of the modernist revolution in the printed book.

In the autumn, back in the city of Tiflis, I got myself taken on as an apprentice by some Caucasian journeyman printers so that I could learn the craft of typography. . . . Obviously, 41° had not been a typographical project. It had been created for the defense and illustration of the zaum language. Working slowly, the following year I left my companions and, dissolving 41° with Kruchenykh and Terentiev, I moved on to the printing house of the Union of Georgian Cities as a client, where, following my indications, the printer Adrien Tiernov executed the [typographical] composition of all the publications of 41° during the years 1919 and 1920, after which I left Tiflis to go to Paris, via Constantinople.[11]

The other important facet of Iliazd's activity during his Russian period can be described under the heading "everythingism." Although we know how impetuously Iliazd attempted to publicize Futurism as a rallying point against the retrograde and obscurantist forces of academicism and outmoded artistic formalism, beginning in November 1913, along with the painter Ledentu and Larionov's group, he began to formulate the tenets of everythingism. In a joint lecture given with Ledentu in Moscow, Iliazd articulated the position Benedikt Livshits later described as the "left flank" of art:

The ego-futurists were our [the Livshits group's] adversaries on the right, while the "Donkey's Tail" and "Target" groups attempted to occupy the left flank in the struggle against us, bearing, in the winter of 1913, the standard of "everythingism." . . . *The basis of everythingism was extremely simple: every epoch, every trend in art, was declared to be of equal value insofar as each is capable of serving as a source of inspiration for the everythingists, who have triumphed over time and space.[12]*

In this statement we should note the temporal dimension of the phenomenon, which included the forms of the past as well as those of the present and future, and we should note also the everythingists' willingness to work with and transform these forms:

It must be stated loudly and clearly that we do not want to burn the cathedrals or the libraries, on the contrary, we rely upon the past; indeed, in our University[13] we are working on all our great classic poets along with our own. We want to

destroy nothing, but rather to create with the materials others have passed down to us.[14]

This radical option enables us to grasp the meaning of Iliazd's modernity as well. One example in this connection is the case of Niko Pirosmanachvili, also known as Pirosmani. What Iliazd perceived in the work of that Georgian folk painter (fig. 3), beyond his "primitivism," was, above all, the modernity of his compositional framework, his reduction of form to geometrical structures, and the plastic qualities of his work, which were equal to those in the Cubo-Futurist pictures of such an artist as Malevitch. Thus the archaic, hieratical character of Pirosmanachvili's animals or human figures makes them prime examples of the articulation of certain givens in modern painting. The same process was reflected in the link between Cubism and African art. In addition, Gontcharova's "neoprimitivism," reflecting an Eastern tradition and advanced by Iliazd, was directly derived from the order of pictorial concerns of a painter like Pirosmani.

And it is to this basic primitivism brought to canvas that Pirosmanachvili owes his dewy perfection, a necessary link between the traditions of the East from which he emerged and the art of a West still seeking its truth. Pirosmanachvili's work sets a valuable example for the painters of a new generation.[15]

Iliazd's artistic experiments within the avant-garde, his alliances and his achievements, formed the basis of a whole field of knowledge and know-how. All of his later interest in printed art and in literature was influenced by this "laboratory" period in Russian art, at a time when options were clear-cut and determinative. After this experience, there could be no turning back. This was what, to a great extent, led to the activities Iliazd engaged in upon his arrival in Paris in 1921. His efforts to re-

Fig. 3. Niko Pirosmanachvili. *The Beautiful Ortatchala.* c. 1913. Oil on waxed canvas, 45¹¹/₁₆ × 18⅞" (116 × 48 cm). National Museum of Georgian Arts, Tiflis. Formerly collection Iliazd

Fig. 4. Iliazd's poster announcing his conference "Les Nouvelles Ecoles dans la poésie russe," Paris, November 27, 1921. Lithograph, 10⅝ × 8¼" (27 × 21 cm). Private collection

establish in Paris the University of The 41st Degree (the association of avant-garde poets he formed c. 1916–17) demonstrate his determination to hold to the modernist path. That determination was made explicit in the series of lectures and events he organized in Paris up until 1923 (fig. 4). During this period his closest alliance was with Dada, which had moved its headquarters to Paris. In spite of this alliance, however, André Germain, writing in 1923 of "Russian *surdadaïsme,*" set Iliazd apart from his Dadaist associates:

He made Messrs Philippe Soupault, Paul Eluard, Tristan Tzara, seem totally outmoded; these waning poets nevertheless showed up this evening to lend support and pay homage to this younger brother who has so cavalierly risen above them, a truly rare gesture of confraternity, for demi-extremists usually dislike nothing more than a super-extremist.[16]

In this regard, two clarifying facts should be mentioned. The first is a letter from Iliazd to Marinetti written in early 1922,[17] which reveals the hesitations, the crisis created by Futurism and the death of Dadaism, a crisis of which Iliazd himself was keenly aware. The second factor underlying this moral dilemma was the notorious "Soirée du *Coeur à barbe*" ("Evening of *The Bearded Heart*"), which degenerated to such an extent that it led to the ultimate dissolution of Parisian Dada. Thus the failure of the University of The 41st Degree to reopen, the schism between Dadaists and Surrealists exacerbated by the failed Congress of Paris of 1922, and Iliazd's ambiguous attitude toward Marinetti all played a part in the rupture in the artistic front and in Iliazd's subsequent isolation. The appearance in 1923 of *lidantYU fAram* ("Ledentu as Beacon"; plates 7 and 8) marked the end of the "flamboyant" cycle of Iliazd's work:

I throw out this book, farewell youth, farewell zaum, farewell

long path of acrobatics, of ambiguity, of cold logic, of everything, everything, everything.[18]

A long silence ensued, not unaccompanied by material difficulties.

THE POWERS OF LANGUAGE: FROM POETRY TO DANCE

Poetry is number, proportion, measure: language—except that it is a language that has turned in upon itself, that devours itself and destroys itself in order that there may appear what is other, what is without measure, the dizzying foundation, the unfathomable abyss out of which measure is born. The reverse of language.
Octavio Paz, The Monkey Grammarian,
English translation, Helen R. Lane

A Quest for an "Other" Language

Iliazd's first efforts in the poetic arena reflected a basic questioning of the powers of language, of the various ways language could, through direct action upon its components, be made to alter the perception/conception of the world. In this context, Iliazd's theater pieces and the evolution of his concept of *zaum* play a part in the modernist concept of poetic language, in which the poet's status gives him the opportunity to investigate the means of his own writing, his own speech. In order to gain a foothold for itself such poetic discourse had to be arrived at "obliquely,"[19] by back routes, not by transparently standing between words and things, but rather by cultivating its depth, its density.

This is what led Iliazd to write: "That is why there are two languages—everyday language and poetic language, each with its diametrically opposed laws."[20] Here, the experiments in *zaum* or transmental poetry undertaken by Khlebnikov, Kruchenykh, and Iliazd can be viewed as a part of the basic questioning of poetic language that began at the turn of the century and became the impetus for a sharp epistemological break, with regard to both the use of poetic language and the elucidation of its derived principles (its laws). Khlebnikov's slogan "the word as such" opened the way for this exploration of a poetic language that had been pulverized, broken down into its distinctive components, its sonoral elements and its innate laws of organization. The process thus brought over into poetic expression was, of course, the sign of and the reason for an ethical and aesthetic crisis in Russia and in Western Europe,[21] and the literary process had corollaries in the plastic arts. Theoretical developments pushed the study of such trends to the extreme, as reflected particularly among the members of the Formalist school[22] and in the positions advanced by the magazine *Lef* ("Left Front for the Arts") and other such publications. The close similarity of the expressed intentions and statements of artists and poets to those of theoreticians is revealed, for example, in such sentences as these by Viktor Shklovsky, lapidary as they may be:

The word in art and the word in life are profoundly different: in life, it works like the beads on an abacus, in art it is textural. We perceive it as sonority, it is pronounced and heard through and through.[23]

In researching and experimenting with this "other" language, a kind of "quest" came into play, essentially a striving to cultivate new "sensations" for the "new man," the *leitmotiv* of the artistic avant-garde in Russia and in Western Europe as well (fig. 5). This quest took two forms: first, research into the principles and laws upon which the new language would be based, which involved an attempt to elucidate the active forces of poetic language (sonority and morphology) and, indeed, to destroy "the logic of an outmoded rationality" (George Kubler) in order to create a "transrational" language; second, growing out of this research, efforts to become fluent in a truly poetic language and to gain access to and control over the irrational forces governing it.

Around this autarky of the word and its sonorous matter morphological laws were invented to underpin the new language: first came *sdvig*, or the theory of distance, of displacement. As Iliazd described it:

Sdvig is the deformation, the demolition of voluntary or involuntary language through the displacement of a part of the word's mass to another place. Sdvig can be achieved etymologically, syntactically, phonetically, morphologically, orthographically, etc. . . . Sdvig is not only the useless result of linguistic deconstruction. Sdvig is also a means of poetic expression.[24]

From this first principle of displacement we move on to the second principle, that of the "itinerary of globality" (or global itinerary):

The itinerary of globality closely follows sdvig by continuing the demolition of logical language "in status nascendi." . . . The itinerary of globality gives rise to unmouthed speech . . . and here the hidden meaning is discovered, not by logical association, but by phonetic association. . . . It is the key to understanding and explaining dreams, as proposed by Professor Freud. Sdvig, the itinerary of globality and unmouthed speech are the three foundations from which the genius of the young masters Kruchenykh and Terentiev has sprung.[25]

Thus the two major poles supporting *zaum* poetry: on the one hand knowledge of the formative laws of phonetic poetry which, notwithstanding the repeated statements of its practitioners, is neither purely nonsensical nor apprehended as the result of the use of pure logic in dissecting the components of language. On the other hand, we have this overflow of meaning which is based on a recourse to neologisms, the sounds of foreign languages, baby talk, and phonemes. The result is a language capable of expressing emotions and feelings that are beyond rationality. This language, conceived as

Fig. 5. Kiril Zdanevitch and Vasily Kamensky. *Ferroconcrete Poem, Tiflis*, from the miscellany *1918* by Kamensky and Alexei Kruchenykh. Tiflis, 1917. Lithograph, 13½ × 9" (34.3 × 22.9 cm). Private collection. This almost purely visual "poem" alludes to a quest to establish Futurist outposts in the Georgian cities of Batumi and Baku.

"the Word in the beginning,"[26] can be viewed as one of the origins of "refound" language.

The unique thing about Iliazd's transmental language was that it created a language/writing fusion, and that fusion revealed the graphic substance, equally fundamental to the phonic substance of "living speech." Let us consider the uniqueness of this poetic language, which was conceived primarily as a theatrical language,[27] one that "stages," that features, as it were, the phone as the motive agent of living speech. This dimension of the phone as one of the constituent elements of Iliazd's *zaum* language can be discerned in the layout of the written language on the page: we find an orchestral ordering of one, two, or more voices, a score, intended—above and beyond its independent and self-sufficient visual voluptuousness—for vocal performance. Orchestral poetry is one of Iliazd's major contributions to the experiments of early-twentieth-century Russian poetry.

The orchestral poem, which I created in 1913, carries forward the task of liberating poetic language in a new direction. We call orchestral poetry that poetry written for several voices simultaneously, each voice having its particular theme. Voices are heard, simultaneously, declaiming either in unison (in chorus) or each a different part. In orchestral poetry, poetic language is wrenched out of its individual framework and finally set free.[28]

Jean Claude Lanne has described Iliazd's theatrical concept of *zaum* as follows:

Zdanevitch's [Iliazd's] detailed annotations, his painstaking glosses of his invented graphic signs, evidence a concern for living speech, for declamation. Thus, ultralogical poetry, transrational dra(ma), is a poetry of declamation. . . . Through its vocal interpretation, the composition done in "zaum" is reinstated as language: the semanticism inherent in every language, in effect, is reconstituted by means of

pauses, modulations of voice, rhythm, inflections, etc. . . . that create a kind of mimetic, gesticulatory, phonic syntax.[29]

The phone is supported first by the score, the written page that controls the emission of the sounds. The other site in which the manifestation of the voice, actual speech, is anchored is the theatrical stage, the pendant of the book, another site of manifestation. That is why Iliazd chose the *dra*(matic) form for his poetic works, to make them reverberate through the assemblage, the "gathering"[30] of the speech preferred. Thus, not content with graphic indications of orchestration and polyphony, the author attempted to achieve theatrical representation, a manifest effectuation of the sonic drama.

In 1916 Iliazd's play *Yanko krul' albanskai* was produced in Stephanie Essen's studio in Petrograd, following the author's directions.[31] And at the outset of his stay in Paris, Iliazd doggedly attempted to have his dramatic poems staged and to supervise their choreography, managing in April 1923 to have *Ostraf paskhi* and *Asel naprakat* performed.[32] Clearly, as a result of these performances, Iliazd's concept of poetic language took on a dimension greater than that of pure sonority. Henceforth, it was broadened to include gesture, the body's "trembling" under the effect of the declamation, rhythms, and movements of the voice, as well as the responses of other individually controlled bodies. We will return to this.

The Modernist Bias, Reviewed and Corrected

These particularities of a poetic language devoid of imagistic metaphor, of the functional semantic transparency of everyday language, this resurgence of meaning through the conjunction of the phone and the graphic sign we find in the *dras*—all this was reflected in Iliazd's poetic activity during his Parisian period. A defensive bias in favor of any innovative path for poetic language was in fact one of the constants of all Iliazd's subsequent activities. At the same time, his belief in the importance of the poetic discoveries made in the early years of the century never faltered, and Iliazd always defended the modernist poets. Indeed, some of his publications afforded him the opportunity to elaborate on the discoveries he had made as a young poet and to link them with those made by other discoverers of a modernist language. Here we should note the importance of the 1949 anthology *Poésie de mots inconnus* ("Poetry of Unknown Words"; plates 12–16), one of the important historic artifacts in any recapitulation and clarification of the course of twentieth-century modern poetry.

Indeed, thirty years after the linguistic experiments carried out by the Russian avant-garde poets, a quarrel between Iliazd and the "letterists," in the person of Isidore Isou,[33] led the publisher/poet to issue *Poésie de mots inconnus* to clearly indicate the derivative nature of letterism and to define its true scope.[34] This anthology, distinguished more by quality than by comprehensiveness, contains the poems of a great many of the people who, in their efforts between 1910 and 1920 to overturn the conventions of poetic language, invented what is now called "phonetic poetry," what Iliazd referred to as "poetry of unknown words." He wrote of the anthology the controversy inspired: "Having amassed samples of forgotten phonetic poetry, I decided to publish *Poésie de mots inconnus*, in which I brought together everything that had been done 25 years prior to letterism."

The pieces Iliazd chose for his anthology, which he ironically publicized under the title *Après Nous le lettrisme* ("After Us, Letterism"),[35] indicate the radical element in his recognition of the true pioneers in phonetic poetry. The larger part of *Poésie de mots inconnus* is devoted to poetic works by the Futurists (Russian) and Dadaists. However, these are presented with poems by Ronké Akinsemoyin (in the Yoruba tongue) and by Antonin Artaud, in addition to other selected works of "authen-tic" sound poetry. Iliazd explained in an editor's note: "This book has been created by Iliazd to illustrate his comrades' cause and in memory of . . ."[36] An additional volume emerged from this desire to defend and give voice to modernist poetry: *Poèmes et bois* ("Poems and Wood"; plate 21), which arose out of the close collaboration between Iliazd and Raoul Hausmann, one of the pioneers of Dadaist poetry.

Iliazd's interest in language games and their salutary usage manifested itself in many and diverse forms. Thus one of Iliazd's last works, *Boustrophédon au miroir* ("Mirror Boustrophedon"; plate 34), gave new life to the ludic nature of poetic activity, which owes as much to the powers of language as it does to the act of writing.[37] In *Boustrophédon au miroir* we have a true effectuation of the poetic language as the labor, combination, *découpage*, gestation of the imposition of words. Here, linking palindrome and boustrophedon, the game of reading becomes one with the game of writing, since the sentences can be read both from left to right and vice-versa.

The considerable labor Iliazd devoted to poetic language in his books made him especially sensitive to innovative writing forms in works of the past. This sensitivity was also a function of Iliazd's everythingist concept of art. And it may form the basis of the Futurist poet's paradoxical admiration for the work of the seventeenth-century Toulousain poet Adrian de Monluc. Iliazd rediscovered and published two of Monluc's texts, *La Maigre* ("The Thin Woman"; plates 17 and 18) and *Le Courtisan grotesque* ("The Grotesque Courtier"; plates 38 and 39).[38] This example deserves going into at some length.

The language (the "tongue") Monluc speaks is of a singular grammatical perfection. There is no revolt against syntax here; the words are correctly ordered in the text. And yet another level of language seems to shimmer through, a "dual sign" language, one that is made particularly evident in the 1630 edition of *Le Courtisan grotesque* by the use of italics. Indeed, the italics serve to emphasize the distance between the fixed syntagm (an accepted expression current in the idiom of a given period) and the narrative, the telling. This diversion of language also sets up a repeated rupture between the descriptive narrative and the order in the discourse emphasized by the constant caesuras, thereby short-circuiting *both* types of discursive convention—that of the prose poem or poetic narrative and that of fixed forms. The relationship of one to the other continually uncouples levels of the text: words play within the text without thereby impeding its progress, which continues as the coherent development of the subject indicated by the work's title.

Thus Monluc was practicing the *sdvig*, or displacement, theory back in the seventeenth century. And indeed, the modernist tendencies prevalent in Iliazd's poetic activities did not prevent him from practicing traditional forms of versification as well. Thus Iliazd's announcement to prospective readers of *Afat* (titled after an Arabic word meaning unhappiness; plate 10)[39]:

Who could have foreseen that in 1938 Iliazd, eternal clown, while revealing his total mastery of Russian metrics, would become the most austere representative of sorrowful and classic poetry? And yet, it is with a work consisting of seventy-two sonnets that today he manifests his contradictory activity. "Afat" will appear as an album decorated with four etchings by Pablo Picasso.[40]

Rahel ("Rachel"; plate 9), too, was a book containing classical sonnets, two of them. The task of classical versification to which Iliazd was now turning his hand took on broader dimensions in his book *Sentence sans paroles* ("Unspoken Sentence"; plate 28), in which, as though responding to a dare, he took up the challenge of working within the constraints of the form known as a "garland," or cycle, of sonnets. The structure of this French sonnet cycle is strictly set: it consists of fourteen sonnets, each with two quatrains and two tercets, and of a fifteenth sonnet made up of the last line of each of the fourteen preceding poems. Iliazd clearly explained the task confronting him in a letter to Matisse, whose collaboration he requested in the publication of his lengthy work.[41] The classical form allowed for a more lyric, elegiac work on the theme of unrequited love, which he had already treated in such mournful tones in *Pismo* ("The Letter"; plate 11). Iliazd was clearly drawn to the linguistic challenge of this poetic form, notwithstanding its classicism: "Iliazd regarded himself as one of the only Russian poets to have succeeded in that rare and difficult sonnet form."[42]

Poetry and Dance

Academic prowess, however, is certainly not the major element of interest in Iliazd's practice of poetry, for his concept of language came to its fullest fruition through dance. Whether in ballet, with its codified positions and steps, or in choreography that had broken with traditional codes, Iliazd's interest in dance had basic links with his interest in poetic discourse:

I've always viewed as remarkable the possibility of setting ballet to poetic recitation, in which each syllable would determine a step, and the acceleration of the vowels, with or without accentuation, would determine their character.

[Ordinary] language does not allow for that because the everyday words, either too short or too long, with too constant a proportion of vowels or consonants, are too feeble to be danced to. However, dance would be possible with abstract "zaum" language. The dance in "Ostraf paskhi" is created in this way.[43]

Indeed, beginning with his earliest poetic productions, Iliazd was experimenting with the relationships between sonority and gesture, breath and movement.

Apart from its theatrical use, abstract language has its raison d'être in dance (its application to dance). The use of abstract language enables us to create rhythms that cannot be achieved by everyday language.

By freeing the sonorous aspect of words from their signification, we enable sonority to determine the character of the movement, which in turn determines the rhythm to which the dancer will dance.[44]

Thus the 1923 performance in which Iliazd, with Lisica Codreano, danced his *Ostraf paskhi* at a soirée devoted to the poet Boris Bojnev.

In his notes for his unrealized ballet *La Chasse sous-marine* ("The Undersea Chase"), drawn up in the late 1940s in a return to the spirit of his *dras*, Iliazd related how he had hoped to get Matisse to design the sets. He also recalled that his seductive gestures while dancing had made the artist laugh:

Ever since the Bojnev soirée I had planned to do a full-length ballet and I wrote "La Chasse sous-marine." That ballet would have fit very well into the context of our exchange of polemics with the letterists. In 1947 I made the acquaintance of Matisse. I went to see him on the Boulevard Montparnasse with my book "Pismo," illustrated by Picasso, to show him my method of laying out a book. Our next meeting was in his apartment in Nice, where, in order to persuade him to give me an engraving for my "Poésie de mots inconnus," I danced for him—he had already gone to bed—and made him laugh.[45]

The same passion for the language of "unknown words" and for the ballet compelled Iliazd to publish a text by a seventeenth-century poet from Toulouse,
René Bordier: *Récit du Nord et régions froides pour l'entrée des baillifs du Groenland et Frizland au grand bal de la douairière de Billebahaut* ("Narrative of the North and the Cold Regions for the Entrance of the Bailiffs of Greenland and Frizland to the Grand Ball of the Dowager of Billebahaut"; plate 20). "This book will afford an opportunity to 'stage' the unique, brief, and totally phonetic passage, with its irresistibly *zaum* consonants, that Bordier created for the entrance of [the characters] Cramail and the Duke of Nemours," Iliazd wrote.[46] This *topinambou* language,[47] probably invented, according to Iliazd, by Monluc (upon whom the Cramail character is most likely based), echoes in its modernity the experiments of the most famous modern-day poets. Moreover, the purely rhythmic sonority of the text, in incantation so well suited for gesture, enabled Iliazd to link poetry and dance, text and choreography, to an unprecedented degree. Iliazd considered Bordier to be one of his most important forerunners in broadening the scope of the poetic act.

Iliazd's interest in the synthesis of these mediums is further reflected in his publication of Jehan-François de Boissière's *Traité du balet* ("Treatise on Ballet"; plate 22), which describes ballet spectacles in seventeenth-century Toulouse. In the afterword of his *Traité du balet* Iliazd makes his publishing motive clear:

Read, friend Reader, this immortal and totally unknown work, as evidence of the happy era when ballets were written and danced by poets.

Another felicitous element that consolidated Iliazd's feelings of kinship toward Boissière and Bordier was the latter's having realized in Toulouse, in the seventeenth century and therefore long before the term itself existed, the alliance of the phonetic poem (*topinambou* language) and dance (ballet).

WRITING(S)

The questioning of language inherent in Iliazd's work and the interest in games such questioning inspired were inevitably accompanied by a fascination with writing. Iliazd's passion for writing expressed itself in a variety of ways, first in his pleasure in deciphering signs, but also in his pleasure in inscription as gesture, as line, as the staging of the materiality of writing, in the graphic sign as a feast for the eye. Here we come to a facet of Iliazd's oeuvre that demonstrates that, contrary to the beliefs of certain structurally inclined linguists and semioticians, not only "form" but also "substance" has import.[48] Furthermore, Iliazd's exposure of his manipulation of medium speaks to one of the fundamental issues in the modernist adventure.

It is illuminating to consider Iliazd's *zaum* writings, particularly his five *dras*, in this regard. The very title of *Yanko krul' albanskai* ("Yanko, King of Albania") indicates a preoccupation with a "foreign" language and its writing, in this case Albanian. Does it matter that there is no *real* correspondence between Iliazd's *zaum* and the Albanian language? In his notebooks Iliazd is careful to make clear that he did not use the terms *zaum* or "transrational language" until "later," during his Caucasian period. He deliberately selected Albania for his title because of its unfamiliarity, its stranger/strange, foreign, and unknown character. Of course at this time he was also searching for an "other" language, an invented language, to use in his poetic activity.

On the other hand, is it really mere chance that Iliazd titled his second *dra Ostraf paskhi* ("Easter Eyeland")? Leaving aside questions of plot, it cannot be wholly coincidental that huge stone blocks appear as important actants (subjects or objects) in the *dra*. Are the monoliths on Easter Island not also the bearers and embodiments of an as yet undeciphered ideographic writing, entities

that have, as such, remained mute in history? There is no doubt that Iliazd maintained this interest in the enigmatic inscription of signs: thirty years after he wrote *Ostraf paskhi* he designed and published the anthology *Poésie de mots inconnus*.

This concern with "ciphered" writing took various forms in Iliazd's oeuvre. In some of the more modest books of the Russian period we can already discern how Iliazd used typographical design to highlight possible readings. His juxtapositions of words in heavy typefaces with words in lighter typefaces can be understood as a form of "hypogram" that introduces "physiognomical features" into the text. This is the third meaning Ferdinand de Saussure attributes to the hypogram, that through which we "emphasize the features of the face with makeup."[49] The very thickness of the letters (heavy or light) in this kind of typographical design allows for different levels of reading. A text so set in type reveals and offers itself to the eye in alternating ways. This manner of "working" the graphic signification of the written text[50] is amplified and made more complex in the final *dra, lidantYU fAram* (1923). Indeed, each page of this book offers itself as a picture, that is, as pure "graphism," exhibiting a typographical repertory so vast that it defies inventory. Furthermore, so playful is its organization that some of the pages virtually defy reading, breaking as they do with the linear conception of the text and forcing the reader to adopt a circular contemplation, to decipher in a back-and-forth manner more appropriate for viewing a picture. One of the important aspects of *lidantYU fAram* is the introduction of "figures," drawings, motifs, into the body of the text itself, which some have attempted to read as rebuses, although they mimic rather than form such puzzles.

Thus the figure and the motif play with the ambiguity of the space they occupy between graphic and phonic representation, giving rise to a perpetual codification that can lead to a new order of meaning. This phenomenon is not in evidence in the early *dra Asel naprakat*, the design of which, extraordinary though it may be, maintains the conventional distinction between illustration and text. Thus in *Asel naprakat* Gontcharova's tiny drawings of donkeys are scattered on the pages as accompaniments to the text, while Iliazd's two typographical compositions are offered as discrete items. The disarticulation of the traditional ordering of writing (or reading) in *lidantYU fAram* challenges the hierarchical relationship maintained between motif and figure, with the former always included within the latter, in the manner of a decorative frieze on a building or a letter in an illuminated manuscript. The allegiance of motif to figure is contradicted in another significant way in *lidantYU fAram* in the relationship between text and pagination. In effect, the page numbers become figures in themselves; they become autonomous and abandon their functional existence on the page through their countless variations in appearance. Far from remaining modestly in the margins, the page numbers move like actors on a stage obeying blocking instructions or some choreographic plan, invading the surface of the page, becoming bodies that move, that change size, thickness, and "type."

All of this suggests that, for Iliazd, writing the meaning-productive act was conflated with writing the act that gives signs their materiality. Thus the act of production, the formation of meaning, occurs by assuming the significance of signs in their specific appearance. Here, too, we note the modernity of Iliazd's attempts to open another semantic field beyond referential illusionism. What was fundamentally at stake for Iliazd in the act of publishing a text was not, strictly speaking, diffusion, but rather the work of giving form, of "in-forming."

In fact, Iliazd had been combining the activities of writing and publishing even in his first book-making experiments in Tiflis, with *The 41st Degree*. This con-

junction of the two practices remained a constant in his later works, a basic element in his concept of publishing as a writing/transcribing synthesis. In this regard two models emerge. First, we have the image of the "scribe"[51] in his social function, writing his text upon the *tabula* (tableau, tablet, table—including the mathematical table), a framed space, a limited surface. The second model is that of the copyist-monk, a faithful transcriber of his text, respecting its conformity, its exactitude.

We know of Iliazd's intransigence regarding respect for what we call the "letter" of the text. It was demonstrated in the many bibliographic investigations he undertook, reflected in the index cards, notebooks, and collated editions that fill his archives. This was the intellectual side of his work. It was accompanied by the material labor, the typographical transcription and layout of the text. Only after this stage could the text emerge in its actual materiality—as matter to be "worked," to be formed.

Thus we travel from the preparatory pages of the *dras* and their graphic orchestration up to Iliazd's last work, *Le Courtisan grotesque*, the apex of the publisher's typographical transcriptions. The example deserves our attention. The many surviving maquettes, experimental plates, and manuscript pages enable us to witness the transformation of one system of writing into another. It is significant that Iliazd chose to base his edition of *Le Courtisan grotesque* on a unique edition published in Toulouse in 1630 that contains italics *in texto*. What impelled Iliazd to opt for this version rather than for the original edition of 1621 (fig. 6)?[52] We may be sure that he was attracted by the play of typographical variation. Of course it would have been an easy matter simply to reproduce this text as it stands, but having virtually renounced punctuation and opted for a typographical style ill-suited for italics, Iliazd was forced to invent. In a superb solution, he rendered the words italicized in the

Fig. 6. Title page of *Le Courtisan grotesque* by Adrian de Monluc. First edition, Toulouse, 1621. Bibliothèque Mazarine, Paris

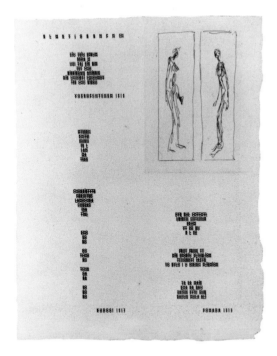

Fig. 7. Alberto Giacometti. Page from *Poésie de mots inconnus* by various authors (this text by Alexei Kruchenykh). Paris, Le Degré 41, 1949. Etching, 12¾ × 10″ (32.3 × 25.4 cm). The Museum of Modern Art, New York. The Louis E. Stern Collection

1630 edition by orienting their letters horizontally, thereby causing the reader to move his body as well as his eyes in the act of reading. Iliazd was thus able to remain faithful to Monluc's text and to his own formal principles at the same time.

The example of extreme typographical inventiveness in *Le Courtisan grotesque* still leaves us with the question of punctuation and its disappearance from Iliazd's books. And here we come up against an astonishing paradox inherent in the articulative structure of the text as conceived by Iliazd. In fact, as Jacques Derrida has written, "punctuation is the best example of a nonphonetic mark in the interior of the writing."[53] Punctuation has a purely visual status; it is the written substitute for vocal inflection in spoken language. A text without punctuation could thus be said to be unreadable. It is only visible. It states itself as purely to be regarded, as a silent visual spectacle on the page, indecipherable if the voice is not brought into play. This paradox in Iliazd's concept of the book decisively severs language from writing, the voice system from the sight system, and sets up a unique exchange between the site of writing (the hand), the site of reading (the eye), and the site of theater (the voice). In this respect, the book *Poésie de mots inconnus* bears looking into. Here, sense no longer commands the rhythm, the declamatory breath. Any reading becomes quasi-acceptable, quasi-valid, until other marks are introduced to guide the process. Thus the accent marks on certain letters in some of Akinsemoyin's poems are indispensable parts of Yoruba language. And on Albert-Birot's page there are dashes indicating the elongation or prolongation of sounds, as well as the following indications at the ends of the three songs that comprise his "poems to be shouted and danced," so closely related to those of Iliazd: 1) prolong the sound; 2) place the hand over the mouth like a plug; 3) form the hand into a megaphone.

In the fragments of Iliazd's *dras* lower- and uppercase

letters are used to accentuate the phonemes. *Poésie de mots inconnus* offers an even richer repertory of relationships between writing, graphic games, and sonority. Consider the remarkable example of Kruchenykh's poems, laid out in long thin columns (echoing Giacometti's slender figures), in a typographical play of overprinted, "trembling" letters, a mode of visual presentation designed to dictate the recitation (fig. 7). The trembling of the voice is an equivalent response, transposed into another medium, of the trembling of the overprinted words. Here, too, we have a masterful demonstration of the power of writing (manuscript or mechanical) to signify, a power derived first and foremost through its visual appearance, its "apparition," something arrived at not arbitrarily, but by design.

Poetry and Number

The example of *Le Courtisan grotesque* also demonstrates how at a particular boundary of elucidation poetry and number become the same, how one cannot exclude the other. Another paradox in Iliazd's concept of poetry and its relationships to language/writing is that this modernist avant-garde poet, through his dissection of the text, carried on a poetic tradition that dates from antiquity. This hypothesis is valid only to the extent that we share the conviction that poetry is as much a matter of number and arithmetic as it is of inspiration and song, and that the poets of antiquity actually did add up, break down, the number of phonemes they employed.

In Iliazd's work the most striking paradox would appear to be the apparent incompatibility between the activity of the "futuristic" poet, totally directed to developing new artistic forms, and the activity of the same knowledgeable and erudite man who tirelessly cultivated the sciences and arts of the past. We seem to observe this relationship to the "antique" character of poetic activity, as described by Saussure, at work in Iliazd's efforts at once to pursue the poetic act and to display it. The presentation of his engendering of the text is made visible *through* his act of re-presenting it.

In all the texts Iliazd published we can observe a concern to obey certain laws of measure, to weigh data and to plumb the character of the work to be rendered. Whether it is a question of separating the text into sections, dividing it into pages, or breaking it down into feet, words, lines, verses, and paragraphs, the process of dispersal and the resultant ordering inevitably involves a "mathesis," the underlying impulse of visual composition.

We would be hard put to find a work in Iliazd's oeuvre that does not reflect this concern, except perhaps *Les Douze Portraits du célèbre Orbandale* ("The Twelve Portraits of the Famous Orbandale"; plate 29) which, oddly enough, consists solely of a series of Giacometti etchings, variations on the portrait theme. Therefore, if we turn again to *Le Courtisan grotesque*, we do so because the procedures involved in the production of that work are so clearly discernible throughout its preparatory stages. Indeed, the preliminary documents and maquettes indicate that the text underwent a total dissection, based on a photocopy of the 1630 edition, in the course of which Iliazd effectively broke every page down into its component letters (its characters). These character-count and copyfitting exercises revealed the number of signs to be dispersed and the space to be filled by them. Here the distribution was controlled by the need for regularity, for homogeneity, for an equal distribution of filled-in spaces and blank spaces, in a nonhierarchical manner, on the space of inscription/appearance.

Typo-ésie

The whole of the typographical realm, in which Iliazd has come to be regarded as a modern master, plays with this concern for writing and its visual appearance, its "tableau" appearance. The innovations Iliazd brought to the modern presentation of text are unquestionably derived from his poetic experiments in the deconstruction of language, in the phonetic and graphic explosion of language, and in elaborating his *zaum*.

[Iliazd] is one of the few people to have understood that the zaum language, in its demand for absolutes, was leading to the metamorphosis of language represented in writing. In his work, the "non-sense" of that extra-logical language was transsubstantiated into a pure, silent graphism that had a pictorial value. The zaum letters, silent, inexpressible, are actually drawings.[54]

In the richness and variety of Iliazd's typographical solutions, in his books as well as his posters, we see displayed before us the materiality of writing. The scope of his invention becomes apparent when we examine *Poésie de mots inconnus*, for example, which demonstrates, among other things, the validity of Paul Klee's dictum "writing and drawing are at bottom identical." A work like *lidantYU fAram*, with its multitude of signs, is another extremely sophisticated experiment in graphic expression, while works such as *La Maigre* or *Le Courtisan grotesque*, with their rigor and reduced number of signs, stand as different but equally convincing examples of an uncommon mastery. A work like *Un Soupçon* ("An Inkling"; plate 33), a short poem by Eluard which in its manuscript form amounts to no more than four lines on a sheet of paper, becomes a monumental edifice through Iliazd's amplifying design and production. Here writing joins architecture and reforges its links with the inscriptions on archaic stelae and encoded monuments. Paradoxically this is the basis of Iliazd's modernity, too.

The question of the medium of writing as reflected in printed books arises because of the way typographical layout can lay bare the conventional reflexes of writing and reading. The most convincing example of this is Iliazd's *Boustrophédon au miroir*. Indeed, historians of

Fig. 8. Iliazd's poster announcing his conference "L'Eloge d'Ilia Zdanevitch surnommé l'ange," Paris, May 12, 1922. Lithograph, 21⅜ × 19⅛" (54.3 × 48.6 cm). The Museum of Modern Art, New York. Arthur A. Cohen Purchase Fund

writing mention the various mediums upon which boustrophedons have been inscribed—stelae and vases, for example. A very large number of ancient writings are in the boustrophedon form.[55]

The idea for *Boustrophédon au miroir* derived from Iliazd's pleasure in writing games. In a letter to Georges Ribemont-Dessaignes of July 1969 Iliazd proposed to his "Deposed Dada Aesop" a "formula for presenting palindromes" in which letters would be reversed—giving the entire utterance a "round trip" effect—and would move not merely from left to right but from top to bottom. Iliazd's obvious interest in this kind of "mirror poetry" gave him an opportunity to renew his links with *zaum*, because the layout he chose caused breaks in discursive continuity. Thus names of friends, authors, and other dear ones begin poems on almost every page of *Boustrophédon au miroir*, but Iliazd also used the name of a ski champion he had never met—"ANNEROSLI ZRYD"—purely for the sake of its uncommon sonority.

The phenomenon of the direction of writing is clearly central to this work. However, we can find even more illustrations of writing's possible orientations in the pages of *65 Maximiliana, ou L'Exercise illégal de l'astronomie* ("65 Maximiliana, or The Illegal Practice of Astronomy"; plates 31 and 32) and *Poèmes et bois*. Intention (concept) and layout vary from one to the other. On certain of its pages the former clearly indicates the movement from top to bottom inherent in the astronomer's act of seeing, suggesting the axes and vectors of his gaze as it shifts from the heavens to the earth. Here, too, the text's physical disposition masterfully reflects the significance of the narrative. And here, too, we find linked in structural balance layout and gesture, scenography and choreography. In *Poèmes et bois*, the vertical orientation of the textual elements in the form of columns can be read as an "oriental" layout, one that calls to mind Chinese or Japanese writing. The same is true of certain pages of

Poésie de mots inconnus, about which one contributor, Hausmann, wrote:

The book is VERY handsome. My congratulations. It's as beautiful as any Chinese or Japanese book, and still totally European.[56]

The ruptures commonly found in the word sequences of Iliazd's texts are sometimes complemented by breaks in the nuclei and even the letters of the words. As early as 1922 Iliazd, in a poster for his conference "L'Eloge d'Ilia Zdanevitch surnommé l'ange" ("In Praise of Ilia Zdanevitch, Nicknamed the Angel"), made use of breaks or displacements of letters within words, producing a troubling, disruptive effect on the reading by means of cracks in the forms of the letters themselves (fig. 8). The process was repeated in *Hommage à Roger Lacourière* (plates 35–37), in which Picasso's text, "Aux Quatre Coins de la pièce" ("At the Four Corners of the Room"), is set throughout in broken lines and letters, matching the wavering of the handwritten engraving it is styled after.

In *65 Maximiliana*, which demonstrates a close collaboration between the painter Max Ernst and the poet/publisher Iliazd, we find another dimension of this phenomenon. Here paleographer joins astronomer in a quest to decipher signs, where Ernst's "writings" recall the constellations of Ernst Wilhelm Tempel, the astronomer/lithographer[57] who realized that signs "inter-respond" and interchange from microcosm to macrocosm. Anything that looks like a hieroglyph makes us want to decipher it, in art or nature. Only through an "acuity of sight" can the system of the universe or the meaning of a work be revealed. Thus the instruments of "optics," understood in its general meaning of that which enables one to see, to see better, can be useful only if they are backed up by this faculty of "the art of seeing": "Great lenses do not make great astronomers," Iliazd once remarked, casually revealing a concept of science and art at once philosophical and political.

The Writing that Utters Only One Name

With regard to the revelation of writing, for Iliazd a subject arousing both fascination and a desire for mastery, the task of deciphering seems to have been fraught with problems arising from another "antique" trait. This, in part, involved the question of the theory of proper names[58] that we can glimpse floating around in the interstices of all of Iliazd's productions. This question of identity, which is revealed by the mark of the name, was certainly one of the obsessive notions that haunted Iliazd's thought.

Olga Djordjadzé and Régis Gayraud, in their study of the *dras*, have shown how this question of reversed identity, always the same and always another, is fundamental to Iliazd's poetic oeuvre. Even earlier, in Iliazd's 1913 book on Larionov and Gontcharova, we find the name of a mysterious author, "Eli Eganebury." To those who questioned his authorship of this early work, Iliazd replied: "Fortunately the pseudonym Eli Eganebury, which I used up until 1919, is, like Iliazd, a coded pseudonym. It is the French reading of the Russian dative form of my name, Zdanevitch, in Russian written Eganebury (which is how the Parisian postman read the mail sent to my father)."[59] Thus this concept of the activity of writing and of poetic discourse as the "second way of being a noun" takes the form of a declension (as was the case with Eganebury). It also takes the form of a *sdvig*, a "sliding" proper to *zaum* practice, which sums up in a single term the operations described by Freud in the work of dream: displacement, condensation, secondary development. This is, indeed, how "Iliazd" itself was created.[60] Based on the transformational principle of *svdig*, a whole series of appearances of the noun be-

comes possible, in an anagrammatic form, particularly following the principles of alliterative poetry.

For example, in Iliazd's fourth *dra, zgA YAkaby* ("As if Zga"), this entire play of identities is at work, on the one hand between Zda and Zga, and on the other hand between the actors in the drama, who are repeated in an infinite play of mirrors. First we have "Zga," "As if Zga," "Mirror Zga," and "As if Mirror Zga," then "Lilith," "Lilia," "Ilia," "Liou," "Lalia," followed by a conflation of both scries. In *lidantYU fAram* we have "Iliazda," which is also present on the poster for "L'Eloge d'Ilia Zdanevitch surnommé l'ange."[61]

Another instance of a borrowed name is found in *Les Douze Portraits du célèbre Orbandale*, the contents of which, a series of etched portraits of Iliazd by Giacometti, is hardly reflected in its title.[62] When his wife asked "Why 'Orbandale'?" Iliazd laconically replied: "Well, after all, I couldn't very well put 'the celebrated Iliazd'!"[63] Obviously, the question of identity and the way in which it occurs and recurs, overtly or covertly, camouflaged, plays an important part in Iliazd's activity and pronouncements. Here we are clearly dealing with an ambiguity. It is difficult to determine whether an impulse for obliteration — the effacing of identity — or a desire for equity motivated Iliazd. He wished to recognize and to "shed light on" those who have been unjustly neglected or forgotten by history, or underestimated by their contemporaries. On this list we find Monluc, Tempel, Roch Grey, and Pirosmani, true stars in Iliazd's constellation. Iliazd cultivated paradox, perhaps in an effort to avoid falling prey to received opinion. His respect for those who have found themselves forgotten is reflected in a maxim he made famous: "To fall into oblivion is the poet's best fate."

And wasn't there something like a recognition of oneself *in* another person operating in Iliazd's admiration for Adrian de Monluc, Baron de Montesquiou, a/k/a

Comte de Cramail (or Carmaing), who used the name "de Vaux" as a pseudonym when signing certain of his works[64] — two of which, *La Maigre* and *Le Courtisan grotesque*, Iliazd published? In a note to the reader in *La Maigre*, Iliazd wrote:

Was [Monluc] not desirous of remaining unknown? The anonymity and diversity of the borrowed names that accompany his writings, the various names and titles he himself used during his life, all helped protect him against the baseness of historical recognition.

Iliazd was also drawn to the poetess/painter Hélène d'Oettingen, who hid behind a series of pseudonyms: Baronne Hélène d'Oettingen, François Angiboult, Roch Grey, Léonard Pieux, and Jean Cérusse.[65] In memory of Roch Grey, "fallen into oblivion," he undertook the publication of *Chevaux de minuit* ("Midnight Horses"; plate 19), a lengthy "epic" poem accompanied by equestrian prints by Picasso.

Iliazd's fascination with name-play is also discernible in *65 Maximiliana*. Consider that the name of the planet in the work's title, referred to repeatedly throughout the text,[66] contains the first names of both collaborators: *MaximIliana*. Further, the painter's family name is the first name of the planet's discoverer (Ernst Wilhelm Tempel). Ambiguity is clearly present in all these effects, the masks and the camouflage used to conceal Iliazd's names and those of his authors. We come to regard it as one of the active wellsprings of any act of writing, as the mark and trace of a primal, original inscription, a search for identity, for a site, for a name.

THE ARCHITECTURAL METAPHOR

In *lidantYU fAram* Iliazd reached a high point in his development of ludic typography as an integral part of the modern page layout; it was a moment of synthesis and a culminating point in his formal experiments. Just as the painters of the early part of the century (the Cubists and Futurists) had striven to introduce words and "concrete" materials into their pictures, so the poets and writers had tried to introduce the "picture" into the text, to produce effects of symbiosis, of hybridization, and to achieve a synthesis of the various languages of art. Modernism meant not only the process of purifying genres but also the exchange and circulation of signs.

In the series of great books he produced during his Parisian period, however, Iliazd adopted a principle of simplified and purified typography, ultimately limiting himself to the uppercase letters of a single typeface. It is as though he felt that proliferation and richness would detract from the structure, the *arche*, the construction of the book itself.

After my departure for Paris, however, I continued to turn typographical problems over in my mind and my search for solutions to them encompassed works not only by Kruchenykh, Terentiev and myself, but also by other practitioners of abstract Russian, as well as foreign, poetry and even rational works,[67] and the whole thing got bound up with a publishing affair that has lasted for fifty years now.[68]

There are constants and continuities in Iliazd's work, but no repetitions. Each of his books bodies forth a new solution, has a form and concept in harmony with the spirit of the work being presented. And each has a layout that seems to embody "the visible trace of the idea."[69] A consideration of the layout patterns of even a few Iliazd books demonstrates his concern for highly refined order. *Chevaux de minuit*, for example, is laid out in an ABCDCDCDCBA pattern comprised of triptychs with illustrations on the center pages, preceded and followed by single-page, *hors texte* illustrations.

Although the clarity and rigor of the end product would suggest otherwise, the structural plan of *Le Courtisan grotesque* went through numerous preliminary formulations before Iliazd arrived at the final layout pattern. An alternation of single-page illustrations printed on the exterior of a folio and double-page illustrations printed on the interior of a folio forms an ABACDC pattern. In order to achieve the perfect balance of the various elements of this system, Iliazd made two complete maquettes for the book, in a reduced format, at the time the precise number of pages and the order of text and illustrations were being established.

As for the construction of *La Maigre*, it was, according to Louis Barnier, done with "totally classical" rigor.[70] To achieve the symmetrical layout of the number of lines he needed, which were to increase to a total of nineteen on a double page in the middle of the book and subsequently to decrease in the same order, Iliazd made use of indentations and blank spaces. Naturally, the spacings between words and letters took on a capital importance. In his unpublished notes he commented:

The search for balance in an isolated letter, no matter how just the proportions one achieves, does not necessarily avoid a crowded, chaotic page; one must begin by using variable spacing between letters to balance the page, by using the simplest of type, devoid of any vestiges of handwritten script, the simplest of verticals. One must begin by spacing out letters that have become overcrowded for reasons of economy and achieve variable spaces by inserting what are called space bars between the letters throughout the line.

I'm well aware to what I condemned myself because of that crazy notion: I've spent hours of my miserable life inserting tiny lead bars between the thousands of letters that passed through my fingers.

To put the idea [of variable spacing] into practice I selected a text by Adrian de Monluc, an unknown but nevertheless the most remarkable of seventeenth-century writers, a victim of the jealousy of statesmen and of the ignorance and prejudice of historians. . . . [It was] "La Maigre," which I urged Picasso to illustrate. . . .

My comrades at the printshop thought I was crazy when they saw me inserting spaces between the letters of a prepared font . . . [but] "La Maigre" revolutionized modern typography. Even if I'd had to spend ten years at the fontmaker's to get the characters to make my pages look right, it's obvious that I've won.[71]

For Iliazd, *La Maigre* represented a well-earned triumph after years of dogged attempts to make "the work" correspond to "the idea." It was the outcome of an attention to detail that reminds us of Plato's remark in *Philebus*: "I mean to say, that if arithmetic, mensuration, and weighing be taken away from any art, that which remains will not be much."[72] Here, on the strength of what we call the architectural metaphor—the edifice and its order, the edifice as a constructed, produced body—layout *becomes* representation and makes visible the spectacle of production, like an exhibited, readable, palpable anatomy. Iliazd turns what has been a rule proper to poetic discourse vis-à-vis meter, number, and rhythm into a constructive principle of the book itself.

The particular way in which the pages are assembled, the manner in which they establish the stressed rhythms by which they should be read, guides us on the journey through the book, which becomes a series of variously laid-out sites. We move through this journey, this itinerary, quickly or slowly according to the density of these sites, or, conversely, according to their openness. The eye is impelled to search out a way among the perspectives spread before it in the "archi-textual" consolidation of the various book pages.

The use of architectural metaphors in describing Iliazd's works and the constructive processes inherent in them arises as much from the material, physical character of his books as from their conceptual elaboration.

And in fact, Iliazd's investigations in the field of Byzantine architecture, the diagrams and plans he made at various times throughout his life, the rigor and graphic quality of his page layouts, only serve to further consolidate this relationship between architect and publisher.[73]

Text/Image Relationships

The demands of Iliazd the architect, the *maître d'oeuvre*, the foreman, have not only been described by the artists associated with his projects; they are also inscribed in the various preliminary stages that preceded his finished books. Anyone examining the maquettes, trial runs, proof sheets, and other accompanying matter of Iliazd's books, from first layout to final volume, quickly realizes the rigor and determination it took for Iliazd to give expression to the "idea." With regard to text/image relationships as well, Iliazd categorically controlled the framing and placement of illustrations. In *Rahel*, Léopold Survage's two woodcuts are arranged around the space that contains the poem (fig. 9). In *65 Maximiliana*, the printing and positioning of Ernst's writings/hieroglyphs were the results of lengthy preliminary work with tracing paper, in which a whole range of reductions and enlargements of the final arrangements of signs was tried. In these graffiti-covered pages the frames formed around the illustrations are measured, imposed, by the rhythm, the breath, the respiration suited to the page itself. In *Poésie de mots inconnus* the various text/image relationships evidence a constantly renewed inventiveness. Thus text and image are sometimes presented discretely. On other pages the image takes up all of the space, like a stage set or backdrop, and the text is superimposed upon it, sometimes standing out against it, sometimes laid out to follow the vectors and contours of the colored set in the background. In other cases the text is inscribed in the border or around the perimeter of the illustration, framing it, surrounding it, and contrasting sharply with

the colored spaces. These poems seem to grow like excrescenses of the images.

It goes without saying that the question of framing, of limits, entails prescribing, obligation. Thus the squared structure Iliazd selected for *Poèmes et bois* led to the invention of a new way of dispersing the text on the page, one that dictated a certain height/width relationship for the letters of Raoul Hausmann's poems. The distribution of the type along horizontal and vertical lines makes the poetry explode visually, scrambles its continuity, and multiplies the possible readings. Iliazd wrote of his inspiration for the design: "Of itself Hausmann's poem asks for this challenge: 'algebra is and remains attractive.'"

The authoritarianism of a *maître d'oeuvre* is thus evident, but was it not the very condition necessary for a project's success? With regard to the affair surrounding the publication of *Sillage intangible* ("Intangible Wake"; plate 27), a poem by Lucien Scheler in memory of Paul Eluard preceded by a "crowned portrait" of Eluard by Picasso, Iliazd wrote: "Such a counterfeiting of publication in order to make it accessible to the multitudes is shocking."[74] Iliazd's position on the subject, as set forth in his personal notes, sheds further light on his unique concept of the book:

To take my pages without understanding that their composition is not mere aesthetics for the wealthy bourgeoisie but an experiment in a new means of expression, [without understanding] that the meaning of a poem changes according to how it is laid out (something of which Mayakovsky, for example, was well aware when he increased the number of lines in his poems by breaking them up), is a vile deed. It's shocking.[75]

And, indeed, the *maître d'oeuvre* clearly emerges in Iliazd's interventionist behavior with regard to the imposition of his vision, his concept, on strong-willed col-

Fig. 9. Léopold Survage. Unpublished proof of illustration for *Rahel* ("Rachel") by Iliazd. 1941. Woodcut, 23⅝ × 16⅛" (60 × 41 cm). Private collection

Fig. 10. Detail of *Libro del conosçimiento*, the anonymous fourteenth-century manuscript upon which part of Iliazd's *Le Frère mendiant, o Libro del conocimiento* is based. National Library, Madrid

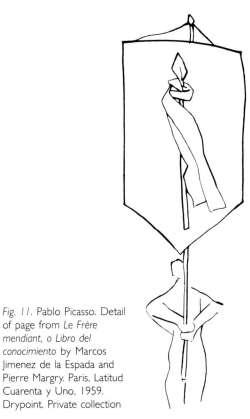

Fig. 11. Pablo Picasso. Detail of page from *Le Frère mendiant, o Libro del conocimiento* by Marcos Jimenez de la Espada and Pierre Margry. Paris, Latitud Cuarenta y Uno, 1959. Drypoint. Private collection

laborators. According to the testimony of Michel Guino, whom Iliazd chose to illustrate *Un Soupçon*:

It took a very long time to produce the book: two years. There were many trials, many drawings, many different states of the drypoints. So very pleasant in life, Iliazd was very dictatorial when it came to work. He was the one who laid out the book. It was impossible to stray very far from his vision, even with regard to colors. He would come to me with little swatches of wool to indicate the color he wanted. He also brought with him impossible demands and a total disgust for half measures or approximations.[76]

In the case of *Hommage à Roger Lacourière* Iliazd even determined the size and placement of the signatures of the work's collaborators. The signature page was measured and laid out by means of an overlay with windows cut into it, which precisely restricted and delimited the spaces for the signatures, eliminating any kind of chance.

Iliazd's correspondence with his collaborators also reveals his skill at convincing the artists with whom he wished to collaborate to illuminate his editions:

Dear Max,

[O]ur world is rife with rumors according to which one of these days some books are going to appear that will be illustrated by you but that won't be mine. I'm reminding you of the promise you once made me that the first illustrated book you would do would be mine and nobody else's. And I continue to believe that you'll keep your promise. With the friendship of your old friend . . .[77]

The adventure of the Miró/Iliazd collaboration on *Le Courtisan grotesque* went on for over twenty years, as we can see from the notes and correspondence between the two men. Iliazd's work is also a lesson in modesty.

Citation

In creating such text/image relationships, as we have noted, Iliazd rarely employed mimetic illustration; at most, he aimed at creating tacit, structural agreements, effective and meaningful reciprocities. The intertextual and intericonographic effects in Iliazd's books must be understood in light of this. Iliazd's intertextual effects were very few. For him, as we have already noted, the text was primary; it took precedence. However, we might mention two books that involve citation. *65 Maximiliana* contains some of Tempel's own data, which Iliazd amassed over years of painstaking research. His sources are set forth in *L'Art de voir de Guillaume Tempel* ("The Art of Seeing of Wilhelm Tempel"),[78] a chronology of Tempel's life published to accompany an exhibition of some of the "good pages" of *65 Maximiliana*. On the other hand, some pages of *Boustrophédon au miroir* list proper names, which in themselves "cite," are references to, some of Iliazd's books: "Marie-Laure," "Adrian de Monluc," "Ledentu," "Claude Garnier,"[79] "Pirosmanachvili."[80]

Intericonographic relationships can be found in the genesis of certain Iliazd works. Thus in *Le Frère mendiant, o Libro del conocimiento* ("The Mendicant Friar, or The Book of Knowledge"; plates 23–26) the appearance of standards and banners is no mere happenstance. They are borrowed directly from the pages of the fourteenth-century manuscript Iliazd used as one of his sources for this narrative of the travels of an anonymous Franciscan (figs. 10 and 11).[81] Aside from the "antique" character such insignia lend the text, enhancing the "long ago" aspect of this story of another place and time, the entire text also "figures"—is lifted on high like a standard, an equivalence, a translation, both in form and in signification—within this "book of knowledge" and, we might add, "of equity."[82] Iliazd raised this book-monument as an homage to that "Castilian mendicant friar":

In the light cast by the past the knowledge of the mendicant friar is admirable and the virtue of his writings gives them actuality. He preaches neither battles nor conversion with regard to the African lands, rich and abounding in all good things, personified by their kings, who equal in their nobility those of Europe and Asia, whether populated by Saracens or by idolators. As for the blacks, they are people of intelligence and understanding. In the Isle of Gropis, it is not the mendicant friar but rather the king who is astounded to see the travelers and to listen to their tales.[83]

If in this instance Iliazd managed to dictate to Picasso the explicit iconographic references he was to work into his drypoints, it is because this "book of equity," as Iliazd called it, was designed to do justice not only to its author but also to the illuminated manuscript enshrining his memory, to his epoch, and to the signs specific to it. Thus this book represents a meeting ground of semiosis and history, as each is read within the other.

The quasi-ritualistic character of these iconic quotations is far from the purely ludic irony in *65 Maximiliana*. In that book the keen-eyed reader can detect scattered here and there amidst Ernst's writings some vignettes that recall the figures in illustrated editions of Monluc and his contemporaries. This manner of linking Monluc with Tempel by using *découpage* and collage was very much to Ernst's taste, and it represents what may be Iliazd's only compromise with regard to the collaboration's Surrealist aesthetic. However, although they may be the most readable, these *découpage* vignettes are not the only citational effects in the book. In fact, some maintain that certain of Ernst's etchings contain explicit references to Tempel's lithographs and conceal a secret correspondence between the cipher of the universe and the written forms of art.

Staging

We have already noted the relationship of Iliazd's works to theater, embodied in the *dras* on a level of declama-

tory poetry, linked with the participation of the voice and orchestration. However, what we are attempting to elucidate here is not only that dimension of the dramatic poem that calls for its representation (in the sense of a theatrical representation), but also the relationship that exists between the dramatic poem and the book as a stage. Thus we can properly read Iliazd's concept of the book as the material construct of a scenario, as a "miniature theater," as he wrote in the dedication of *Asel naprakat*.[84]

Scenic creation is achieved in a more or less complex fashion, and the performance is not to be read in the text or the images alone but in everything that gives the work its materiality. Thus the book's slipcase, its binding, its cover, its front- and back-matter, the folding and unfolding of its pages—all serve to produce effects of meaning proper to the theatrical metaphor (fig. 12). The "support," the accord created between text and image, creates a meaning in and of itself, rather in the manner of a plan of action drawn up to condition or control an attitude, a predisposition, in the reader-spectator who is faced with the object-book. In this sense, the dimension of the object-book is transmuted into a book-site, the site being that of appearance and disappearance.

Decor

The "scenic" concerns reflected in Iliazd's books are given concrete form by the importance accorded the effective and effectual materiality of their "decor": "a welcoming and contemplative cradle," in the words of Jean Leymarie.[85] The construction of the *hors texte* elements of the books—their slipcases, covers, blank leaves, title pages, page layouts, everything that borders, encloses, circumscribes the active deployment of the texts/figures—is an integral part of this staging effect. Thus the proportions chosen, the dimensions decided upon that "limit," that "frame," the performance, deter-

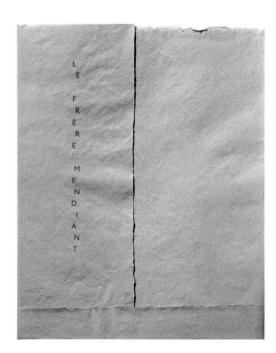

Fig. 12. Iliazd. Cover for *Le Frère mendiant, o Libro del conocimiento* by Marcos Jimenez de la Espada and Pierre Margry. Paris, Latitud Cuarenta y Uno, 1959. Typographical composition, 16⅝ × 13½" (42.2 × 34.4 cm). Private collection

mine the entire scope of the effects on the spectator-reader. A concern for materials was essential in these refined constructive relationships, and Iliazd chose and collected papers and parchments with great care.

He judged a paper not only by its texture, its coloring, and its thickness, but also by the pleasure he took in looking at it and touching it, as if the material had a sensual super-presence. It is easy, for example, to see the sensory relationships at play in *La Maigre* between the china paper on which it is printed, the fineness of its thin, skinlike binding material, and the solidity and consistency of the text's layout. Iliazd arranged alternating colors and textures to set up contrasting or complementary juxtapositions, sometimes creating a cameo effect. The mustard pages that enclose the japan-paper body of *Sentence sans paroles* illustrate this. In *Le Frère mendiant* the contrast between the front-matter leaves of beige Auvergne, gray, and white Auvergne and the white ancient-japan paper of the book's heart gives the assemblage an astonishing monumentality. Iliazd also made use of found paper, hence the butcher's paper in *65 Maximiliana* and *Pirosmanachvili 1914* and the "blue candy paper" dust jacket of *Boustrophédon au miroir*.

We need only read the entries in François Chapon's catalogue of Iliazd's works to realize the importance of materials in the creation of a suitable decor. *Rahel* and *Un Soupçon* both attest to this metamorphosis of the text's appearance. In the first, Iliazd's two sonnets are set within a framework created by Survage's woodcuts, which sometimes attain a width of fifty-three centimeters. In the second, Eluard's poem, which is a mere four lines in manuscript, is transposed and transmuted by the amplitude of a scenic plan that encompasses fourteen pages. This monumentality of effect, along with the parchments used for the layers of coverings, with their amber or bronze surfaces and their varying opacities, gives the

whole supporting structure the solidity of a body contained below the surface of a skin, with all its folds and wrinkles.

The Curtain Effect

These random examples only serve to indicate elements that are common to each of Iliazd's books, from a scenic construction designed to elicit anticipation for what is about to be revealed on stage, to the raising of the curtain. This phenomenon of anticipation, the blank that precedes the actual appearance of the "verb," the "figure," is like the moment when the audience sits murmuring in expectation of a theatrical event about to happen. Thus the covers, the many blank pages of front-matter, the title page—all precede and predispose. They are there to whet the reader's appetite.

On the other hand, the rhythm of waiting, of receiving, established by the matter that precedes the body of the representation itself sometimes follows a plan that demands the increased participation of the spectator in the unfolding of the spectacle. Such is the case with *Chevaux de minuit*, where the structure of the pages, which are folded in thirds, makes it necessary for the reader to go through an unfolding process in order to reveal the figures and the text. The act of reading is thus ordered not only by having to turn pages, but also by having to unfold and refold those pages. The performance is dictated by a predetermined gesture. The same is true of *Poésie de mots inconnus*, an uncut book of quarto pages (fig. 13), each of which must be unfolded in turn, calling to mind acts consisting of a certain number of "tableaux" (in the theatrical meaning of the term). The time factor is thus brought into play. This whole process is in no way arbitrary. Measuring and controlling the desired effect in each case, the plan of each work follows a different formula. In a letter to Matisse concerning *Sentences sans paroles*, Iliazd wrote:

Fig. 13. Poésie de mots inconnus by various authors. Paris, Le Degré 41, 1949. Twenty-seven prints of mixed mediums, 6½ × 5¼" (16.5 × 13.3 cm) (sheets folded in quarto). Private collection

NE COUPEZ PAS MES PAGES

Here is a maquette in which the first leaf containing two sonnets is folded in thirds and in which the second, folded in half, raises the curtain on the illustration.[86]

Whereas the pages preceding the text and the layout of the figures are designed to condition the reader's attitude, leading to the crescendo of the performance's beginning, the blank pages at the conclusion of the book, preceded by the colophon page, bring things to a close. They represent a time for the reader-spectator, still dazzled by the performance that has just ended but which is still vivid in its echoes and reverberations, to recover himself.

Lighting

This manner of setting the stage included lighting effects, shadows and light, and colors designed to create a theatrical atmosphere. Iliazd was exploring these possibilities even in his first *dras*. In *zgA YAkaby*, for example, we find the following elaboration of a luminous ambience:

Z. took great pains with the layout of "Zga": tissue papers in various shades of mauve were laid between the pages, darker for the pages in which Zga has barely awakened . . . to accentuate the mystery, and at the end, when Zga falls back to sleep, whereas the lighter shades were placed in the middle part of the book.[87]

A similar phenomenon is evident in Boissière's *Traité du balet*, in which de Noailles's etchings mimic the effects of projected light and shadow. In this work there is a constant alternation of white/black plates that complements the daytime or night-time entrances of the characters in the narrative. Thus a counterpoint is set up between the illustrations and Boissière's text. In *Traité du balet* we witness the progress of a veritable shadow play, in which the figures stand out sharply in either black or white as if projected against a contrasting backdrop.

The relationships with shadow theater suggested by such devices can be seen as well in the stagings of the texts themselves, in their typographical layouts. In *lidantYU fAram*, for example, some of the pages allow the letters to create shade, to cast shadows, here reminiscent not only of theatrical lighting effects but also of pictorial representation. In *Poésie de mots inconnus* entire pages are arranged so as to reveal the device used to produce the lighting effect. The colophon page, for example, through the play of superimposition in black and red, mimes the actual techniques of stage lighting, producing effects of dual emanation, a reverberation of words and shadows concentrated at the center of the page or spread out to its periphery. This creation of lighting effects by using the physical substance of the book itself, made concrete at the level of form, of expression, reinforces Iliazd's signature concept of throwing light on his subject, of "elucidating."

This labor of production that is perceptible at the various levels on which we read the composition of a book is also evident in the "metaphorization" of the graphic signs into "figures" or "actors" that evolve in space on the page. We have already noted the choreographic positionings used in a work like *lidantYU fAram*, in which writing and theatricality intermingle. In this book letters, individualized or arranged in rows, in columns, obey changing rhythms and move like actors to form multiple configurations. Whether we have a "classical" arrangement, as in *La Maigre*, or a "baroque" composition, as in *Un Soupçon*,[88] the graphic signs are arranged, "place themselves," according to the specific role they are to play in the scenic plan preestablished by the director, the layout artist, as a part of the staging—time, space, actors—within the site of representation. The arrangement of figures (letters, words), their configurations and the rhythms they establish, thus control a respiration, a concentration, made visible. The spaces created between letters, between words, the assemblages or dispersals they produce, all indicate some specific reception. "The blank is a time, a duration, sometimes an eternity," as Paul Claudel said.[89] Thus this play of continuities and ruptures in the development, the spatial displacements of the actors-signs on the page, articulates the effects of a specific ordering of the text and ensures the act of "seeing poetry." To paraphrase Klee, paths for the gaze have been laid out in the work. The text is thus turned into a drawing, a spectacle, a vision superimposed upon the reading itself and on the deciphering of its meaning. Such Iliazd works are synthetic forms, in which word, sight, respiration, book, and theater commingle.

VOYAGE . . . GEOGRAPHY

Iliazd's work unfolded under the aegis "Voyage," voyage into far—imaginary or real—countries, and grew out of a notion of "site," of sites traversed by the perpendicular of time. Voyage and geography are first embodied in the emblem, the cipher, the sign Iliazd deliberately selected to signify his works and his field of activity. This was The 41st Degree, whose university he had hoped to reopen upon his arrival in Paris in 1921. As Iliazd explained later, the number was symbolic: "It is at 41° that most of the great cities of light—Madrid, Naples, Constantinople, Peking, New York—are located."[90]

Further, in launching his appeal to reestablish his University of The 41st Degree in Paris, Iliazd described the projected organization as consisting of:

A society for the building and exploitation of the world's political ideas—Peking, Samarkand, Tiflis, Constantinople, Rome, Madrid, New York. Sections at: Paris, London, Berlin, Moscow, Tokyo, Los Angeles, Teheran, Calcutta. Universities—producing books, newspapers, plays and farms useful for the progress of the idiot literate. 41° is the most powerful organization in the van of the avant-garde in the field of poetic industry. Its beginnings go back to the first decade of this century when, thanks to the work of its collaborators and pioneers, there were discovered in various parts of the terrestrial globe extremely rich and unexplored areas of language. At the present time, 41° embraces more than sixty linguistic systems, including new territories, and attracts new capital with each succeeding year.[91]

Iliazd's text is highly ironic in its enumeration of the "sections" of The 41st Degree throughout the world and the successes achieved by The 41st Degree "society." Its tone and global perspective recall Dada. Although he could joke about the discourse employed in the project, the "society," we should nevertheless not be blind to Iliazd's seriousness with regard to its significance. In *Le Frère mendiant*, for example, instead of a publisher's name we find the phrase "latitud cuarenta y uno," as if it were not only a name, but also a site.

At the center of the reciprocal conjugation of names and sites, we find the narrative of the ascension of Kaçkar Daği (which Iliazd knew as Mount Katchkar), a mountain-climbing expedition Iliazd undertook in 1917.[92] This narrative exemplifies the close relationship that existed in Iliazd's mind between language and territory, between toponymy and geography, between language and politics, and in this respect it is highly instructive. In addition, it underlines the sociohistorical and political range of Iliazd's concerns from an early age, which resulted not from secondhand, received opinion but from broad personal experience.

I had to finish the next-to-the-last of my self-assigned tasks. To reach the summit by way of the Erinenhaven pass, where no traveler had ever before gone, and climb Katchkar, virgin, as I then supposed, the highest peak of the Pontiyski ridge. From there, I expected my eyes to be able to embrace the country I had just traversed, as well as the surrounding areas of the massif, the elevated area of the peaks, to sort out topographical questions peculiar to the site, and, after I had noted the geographical results from my vantage point, it was also my intention, while I had the chance, to gain some understanding of the nomenclature of the central nexus of the Pontiyski ridge, of its freezing, and to collect information about the Khemines and the Christians, as well as the trials experienced by the Georgians of Armenia-Keveka.[93]

For Iliazd, the voyage represented a search for knowledge, a means of taking measure of the equity and inequity of mankind. Such knowledge could not be attained without abandoning the contempt for geography all too common in our time. Even languages cannot be understood without some knowledge of the sites in which they are or have been spoken.[94]

The relating, the narration, of this expedition transcends mere anecdote. It reveals a major point of interest that underlies Iliazd's whole concept of the book. And in fact there is a rapport between language and geography in all of Iliazd's works. Thus in *Le Frère mendiant*, the "book of knowledge," which begins with a preface in "Castilian" and continues in French and Spanish, the naming of names seems to trace the perimeter of the African coastline. We know the lengths to which Iliazd went in trying to shed light on the geographical/historical data suggested by the narratives of the mendicant friar.[95] He collected geographical maps and bibliographical documents, attempting to arrive at precise places, dates, and names.

From the little I know about this map, thanks to the book by M. Texeira da Mota, "Toponimos de Origem portuguesa na Costa Occidental de Africa, Bissau, 1950," I have been unable to accept either the date of circa 1471 given by M. Fontoura da Costa, or even that of 1482 (prior to the building of the Minna Castle) given by M. Texeira da Mota. I put it later than 1490 because of the presence of the name "Cap Saint-Paul."[96]

The establishment of the toponymy of the various maps he consulted in connection with *Le Frère mendiant* represents an amazing body of work, given the few tangible traces of it that appear in the finished product. These are summed up in the following brief passage:

We are attempting neither to lend credence to the narrative nor to rekindle an old dispute, but in the few lines the mendicant friar devotes to the kingdom of Amenuan, of which the Anmines gods and the Minnas are all that remain, how can we fail to recognize the country inhabited by the Akans, the land where, a century later, the Portuguese were to discover the Minna de Ouro, the land once known as the gold coast and now transfigured into the Republic of Ghana. The two arms of the river that flow beyond the country and which are no more than two days apart must be the Afram and the Tano. The name Euphrates given the sacred river that flows through the kingdom is obviously suggested by Bosom Pra.[97]

This passion for geography as reflected in nomenclature and all it represents is one of the foundations of *Le Frère mendiant*. Picasso's airy plates possess the amplitude, the measured respiration, that is appropriate for a narrative about exploring the continent of Africa, which is masterfully evoked in landscapes, figures, and flora. The density of the text is relieved by these vast spectacles, in which the immensity of the landscape can be read in the welcoming spaces created by the painter's incisive line.

The concept of and production work done on *Le Frère mendiant* evidence Iliazd's strong thirst for knowledge, his need to elucidate every question. The dimensions of Iliazd's quest are reflected in the other forms of "voyaging" in his work. If geography is one of the foundations of knowledge, it can also, therefore, symbolize, in voyage form, the opposite of knowledge, i.e., the unknown, those things that are difficult and strange to apprehend, to feel. The "love of geography and culture"[98] is also a way of dreaming, of thinking of faraway and distant places.

Does this evidence a secret fondness for the old-fashioned romantic notions and dreams of getting away from it all? Perhaps, and in Iliazd's case the voyager's desire takes the form of a quest, of quest and conquest, of love, of woman, of knowledge—the wellsprings of all romantic imaginings. The cycle entitled *Aslaablitchia* ("Dunkeyness") can thus be read as the effect created by the man's disguising himself as an animal, "signifying the blindness love causes."[99] Connections with faraway places, the Albania of *Yanko krul' albanskai* and the Easter Island of *Ostraf paskhi*, are also indicative of a mode of thought inspired by the "quest for a desirable object," "woman and the end of the world, the two symbols of the quest."[100]

However, the romantic element in that evocation is to some extent curbed and coexists with material and concrete thoughts about sites and routes. Thus, the rapport of travel and geography is not merely to be found in the exterior, around the edges, as it were, of the books, or merely referentially. It is woven throughout their interiors as well; it forms the shape of the writing. "Writing has nothing to do with signifying, but rather, with surveying, mapmaking, even of not-yet-existent lands."[101] That statement holds true in the case of *Le Frère mendiant* perhaps more strikingly than in the other works. But to say that is to look at things on a superficial level. Perhaps, indeed, any book, as soon as we "conceive it as such," relies upon some kind of geometry/geography.

Thus on any page of *Le Frère mendiant* we can read the sinuous outlines of the coast through the initial letters of each line, their slight or radical unevenness creating for the navigating eye the entrances to grottoes, lagoons, steeply rising cliffs—and, beyond, the vast spaces of the horizon and the sea. Paragraphs, indentations, the un-

evenness and gaps of the lines—all constitute the cartography of the page, its geomorphology, the material of a spatial and topical representation. Such voyages and travels by the eye along hitherto unknown paths are not induced solely in books with "geographic" themes. They are also compelled in *65 Maximiliana*, with its starry skies, the beams falling from heaven to earth. In *Chevaux de minuit* the eye is beckoned by the abysses, torrents, waterfalls, and cavalcades, and the epic is also a history of names, of conquests, and of territories. The typographical layout of *Hommage à Roger Lacourière* is at once an image of a slope and a stairway made visible—an explicitly designed coincidence of the site referred to in the narrative and the image of the site suggested by the text's constructive structure:

Lacourière's print shop was located at the top of Montmartre at the foot of the statue of the knight, since removed.

Built as a banquet hall at the time of the World's Fair, the prismatic building is still crouched against the stairway on the slope.

Beyond the metaphoric play between space and voyage, page and landscape, the notion of site is essentially poetic in nature. It is by means of a language that we penetrate a land, and it is also by means of language that we penetrate a book.[102] In *65 Maximiliana* the text's German, French, and Italian idioms create a journey that is as much geographical as biographical, an itinerary that immediately evokes Tempel's surroundings and the ups and downs of his life. The story of a name can just as well be told by the naming of its surroundings.

Thus Pirosmani is cited by Tiflis, and vice versa. Ledentu, dead, is rediscovered in the name given a mountain crag in the Pontics chain. Monluc is irrevocably associated with Toulouse, and so on. For Iliazd, the dictionary of names is the exact replica, the mirror, the spitting image of the geographical atlas.

Notes

1. Olga Djordjadzé, "Ilia Zdanevitch et le futurisme russe," in *Iliazd*, catalogue of exhibition, Musée National d'Art Moderne, Centre Georges Pompidou, Paris, 10 May–25 June 1978, p. 9.

2. Annick Lionel-Marie, "Iliazd, Facettes d'une vie," in *Iliazd*, op. cit., p. 44.

3. Vladimir Markov devotes considerable space to this in *Russian Futurism: A History*, University of California Press, Berkeley and Los Angeles, 1968. In addition, a number of exhibitions, both in Europe and in America, have in the past several years contributed to unearthing this mass of hitherto unknown artistic material.

4. "Beginning in 1913, the two manifestos signed by Khlebnikov and Kruchenykh quickly became watchwords: "The Word as Such," and "The Letter as Such." For an important study of the close relationship of poetry and painting, see Jiri Padrta, "Malevitch et Khlebnikov," in *Opus International*, no. 69 (Autumn 1978), pp. 70–81 (translated from the Czech by V.L.).

5. "It was at the Trotsky Theater, at a meeting organized by the Union of Youth, that I presented the meeting with the Futurist manifesto on 10 January 1912, fifty years ago now. The next day, every young person's group of every tendency became 'Futurist.' Iliazd, "Fifty Years Later," unpublished notes. Archives Iliazd.

6. Cf. Eli Eganebury (Iliazd), *Natalia Gontcharova/Mikhail Larionov*, Editions Tz. A. Munster, Moscow, 1913.

7. Mikhail Larionov, *Une Avant-Garde explosive*, texts translated, collected, and annotated by M. Hoog and S. de Vigneral, Collection Slavica/Ecrits sur l'art, Editions l'age d'homme, Lausanne, 1970.

8. For this important question, see V. Markov, *Russian Futurism*, and R. Gayraud, "Un Recueil inédit attribué à Il'ja Zdanevic," *Cahiers du monde russe et soviétique*, vol. 25, no. 4 (October–December 1984).

9. Archives Iliazd.

10. The fifth *dra, lidantYU fAram* ("Ledentu as Beacon"), was not published until October 1923, in Paris.

11. Iliazd, unpublished notes.

12. Benedikt Livshits, *L'Archer à un oeil et demi*, translated, with a preface and notes, by E. Sebalt and V. and J. C. Marcadé, Collection Slavica/Ecrits sur l'art, Editions l'age d'homme, Lausanne, 1981, p. 183.

13. Reference to the University of The 41st Degree, which Iliazd founded with Kruchenykh and Igor Terentiev c. 1916–17. Iliazd planned to reopen the "university," dedicated to the advancement of avant-garde poetry, in Paris upon his arrival there in 1921.

14. Interview with Iliazd. Cf. Raymond Cogniat, "Un Laboratoire de poésie/L'Université du Degré 41," *Comoedia*. Paris, 4 December 1921.

15. Iliazd, *Pirosmanachvili 1914*, Le Degré Quarante et Un, Paris, 1972.

16. André Germain, "Ilia Zdanevitch et le surdadaïsme russe," *Créer* (Liège), January–February 1923, p. 135.

17. Archives Iliazd.

18. Unpublished text by Iliazd, Paris, 1923.

19. Michael Riffaterre, *Sémiotique de la poésie*, translated from the English by J. J. Thomas, Collection poétique, Editions du seuil, Paris, 1970, p. 11: "Poetry expresses concepts obliquely."

20. Lecture by Iliazd at his conference "Les Nouvelles Ecoles dans la poésie russe," delivered in French on 27 November 1921 in Paris at the home of Mme Olénine d'Alheim, transcribed by Mihail Tamantchef and edited and corrected by Régis Gayraud (1984). Unpublished. Archives Iliazd. We note that Gayraud is at present preparing a doctoral thesis on Iliazd's poetic work at L'Université de Paris-Sorbonne, under the supervision of Michel Aucouturier.

21. We shall not go into the relationships between the Russian discoveries and innovations and those being made in France, Italy, or Germany, nor shall we discuss which came first, but it is obvious that this "spirit of the times" was prevalent, in a contemporary and parallel way, throughout Russia and Western Europe at approximately the same period.

22. Particularly with Eichenbaum, O. Brik, and, on the other hand, with Shklovsky.

23. Viktor Shklovsky, *La Marche du cheval*, Edition champ libre, Paris, 1973, p. 96.

24. Iliazd. Unpublished notes on conferences, 1922–23. Archives Iliazd.

25. Ibid.

26. Ibid.

27. "At the end of 1916, I had one of my plays, *Yanko krul' albanskai*, performed in Petrograd, and I invented transmental theater." Iliazd, "Les Nouvelles Ecoles dans la poésie russe," op. cit.

28. Ibid.

29. J. C. Lanne, "De Certains Problèmes de traduction poétique particuliers au langage zaum," article submitted to the Centre de Méthodologie du Département d'Etudes Slaves, Université de Bordeaux III, March 1980 (text in the Archives Iliazd), p. 14.

30. "In order to emphasize the primitive side of his theatrical work, in which he returned to the folk tradition of a phonetic language, Z. used to refer to it as "cradle" language (*vertep*), evoking the Ukrainian puppet theaters seen at fairs, very widespread in the sixteenth and seventeenth centuries, whose repertoire included Christmas mystery plays and folk plays about events of daily life." Cf. Olga Djordjadzé, op. cit., p. 16.

31. Cf. Iliazd, unpublished notes on Mané-Katz, 1962, quoted in A. Lionel-Marie, op. cit., p. 50.

32. Cf. Annick Lionel-Marie, op. cit., p. 55.

33. In this connection, see A. Lionel-Marie, op. cit., p. 65.

34. In order to give some of the flavor of these polemics, we include here a part of an article by Pierre Minet (a staunch supporter of Iliazd) that appeared in *Combat* on Friday, 18 July 1947, as well as a passage from Isidore Isou's reply, published on the same day on page 2 of the same newspaper.

Pierre Minet: "Letterism attacks nothing and nobody: it has as much to do with true armed poetry as the strategies cooked up in the Café du Commerce have to do with the art of soldiering. A game, a recipe, original, yes, but that's not much, for accommodating the alphabet. The stupidest, clumsiest attempt at despiritualization ever attempted. 'We're innovators, we're pioneers,' the young cry. We agree! Pioneers of the new banality, bards for robots."

Isidore Isou: "And choicest of all: the latest number of this sinister rag, which can't seem to find any pedants handy when it comes to explicating Guy Vallot's letterist painting but which weekly fills its front pages with filth aimed at us, includes, as an ultimate example of foolishness, an open letter addressed to us. By such means a former plagiarist of Futurism (who did not even have the honor of introducing it into Russia, that task having been performed by Khlebnikov and Mayakovsky), and who then became an imitator of Dada following a forced baptismal article by Ribemont-Dessaignes (and printed at the author's expense), evidently piqued at the silence, indifference and oblivion that have greeted all his poetic tribulations for the past forty years, is hoping (prior to his demise and after twenty more years of silence) to return to literature with a bang. Further, with his conference 'After Us, Letterism'—the very title of which would have already provoked us to come to blows were it not that the man has one foot in the grave already because of his age and the funereal aspect of his 'oeuvre' (sic)—he (of all people) maintains that he is the creator of letterism."

35. See the back of the cover of the preface to *lidantYU fAram* by Georges Ribemont-Dessaignes (1923), which was refurbished with an ocher cover for its redistribution on the occasion of the letterist debate. Iliazd also gave a conference in June 1947 under this title.

36. Iliazd, ed., *Poésie de mots inconnus*, Le Degré Quarante et Un, Paris, 1949, p. 2. The participating poets, in alphabetical order, were: Akinsemoyin, Albert-Birot, Arp, Artaud, Audiberti, Ball, Beauduin, Bryen, Dermée, Hausmann, Huidobro, Iliazd, Jolas, Khlebnikov, Kruchenykh, Picasso, Poplavsky, Schwitters, Seuphor, Terentiev, and Tzara. The artists who contributed illustrations are listed in the Catalogue of the Exhibition, no. 30.

37. According to information furnished by Hélène Iliazd, the readers of the newspaper *France-Soir* were all busy with a "contest" in the form of a literary game for several months in 1955. Iliazd amused himself by collecting on index cards the palindromes sent in by readers. When he reestablished contact with Georges Ribemont-Dessaignes in the late 1960s, the idea for a work on palindromes came up, and Iliazd got his friend to write a preface for it. The palindrome was later replaced by the boustrophedon. For Iliazd, this afforded an opportunity to rediscover an unexpected *zaum*.

38. Iliazd established the biography of Monluc, who signed his works with the pseudonym "de Vaux." The biography was published by A. Coron in *La Vie intellectuelle à Toulouse au temps de Godolin, Quelques Aspects*, Bibliothèque Municipale de Toulouse, October 1980, pp. 101–55.

39. *Afat*, seventy-six sonnets by Iliazd with six copperplate engravings by P. Picasso, Paris, Le Degré Quarante et Un, 1940. This was a "collection of poems on nature, poems dedicated to Picasso, to Chanel," cf. A. Lionel-Marie, op. cit., p. 63.

40. Subscription pamphlet written by Iliazd himself for his first book published in France (1940) after *lidantYU fAram*, which had appeared in 1923. Picasso's collaboration in this work was the beginning of a fruitful friendship; the two artists went on to produce a series of works together.

41. In fact, the book was not done with Matisse, who died in 1954, but with Braque and Giacometti. In addition, according to notes and data in the Archives Iliazd, there were several versions of this garland of sonnets, the first dated 1947, with further reworked versions dated 1959, 1960, 1961, and 1962.

42. A. Lionel-Marie, op. cit., p. 77.

43. Iliazd, "Fifty Years Later," op. cit.

44. Interview with Iliazd by Pierre Minet, 1946, Archives Iliazd.

45. Iliazd, unpublished notes.

46. A. Lionel-Marie, op. cit., p. 71.

47. Language "created on the basis of the language of some Indians brought to King Louis XIII from the island of Maragnon by François de Razilly, Lieutenant-General of Brazil, a colony he vainly attempted to found in 1613," ibid.

48. Here, we use the terms "material," "form," "substance," in the sense employed by L. Hjelmslev.

49. Jean Starobinsky, quoting Saussure, in "Les Anagrammes de Ferdinand de Saussure," *Mercure de France*, February 1964, p. 246.

50. We employ the concept of "work" in the *sdvig* sense described by Iliazd, a sense incontestably related to the Freudian notion of the work of dream as deformation, reconstruction.

51. Iliazd personally dubbed himself with this epithet and claimed to be a "Man of Letters." Cf. the draft of a letter to the organizing committee for the Twelfth International Congress for Byzantine Studies, Belgrade, 16 January 1961. Archives Iliazd.

52. Iliazd does mention at the end of the work that the text was established on the basis of both editions, 1630 and 1621. However, we know that the 1630 edition was the decisive one, the earlier edition having served only as the basis for a few minor changes.

53. Jacques Derrida, *De La Grammatologie*, Collection critique, Editions de minuit, Paris, 1967, p. 323.

54. J. C. Lanne, op. cit., p. 2.

55. See, in particular: F. Lenormant in Darembert and Saglio, *Dictionnaire des antiquités grecques et romaines*, 1962, "Alphabet" article, and Marcel Cohen, *La Grande Invention de l'écriture*, Librairie Klincksieck, Imprimerie Nationale, Paris, 1958.

56. Letter from Raoul Hausmann to Iliazd dated 30 January 1951.

57. "Do you know anyone rich and noble who'd like to help me for a year so that, in Marseilles, independent of lithography, I can further my astronomy studies? Working day and night is too tiring.

Here I'm often out from seven in the evening to four in the morning in the damp cold air and I'm beginning to feel it." Letter from Tempel to Hummel, 1859, Eichhorn, *Natura Lusatica* 5, Bautzen, 1961, quoted in Iliazd, *L'Art de voir de Guillaume Tempel*, published to accompany an exhibition of *65 Maximiliana*.

58. " 'Poetic discourse' is thus but a word's second WAY OF BEING: a developed variation that can make visible, for a perspicacious reader, the obvious (but dispersed) presence of the conductor phonemes." In fact, this phenomenon, which is not solely the property of sacred hymns to the gods, is so widespread that Saussure claimed to have noted it throughout antique poetry—a widespread phenomenon nonexplicit in its causes, albeit almost invariably observable. Cf. J. Starobinsky, op. cit., p. 247.

59. According to Iliazd, the identity of the book's author was always concealed by Larionov, who did not hesitate to take advantage of the fact on many occasions. In 1963, at the opening of an exhibition at the Galerie Zak, in the face of the doubt and incredulity of the art critic Waldemar George, among others, Iliazd found himself obliged to go to considerable lengths to convince people of his authorship of the book. Cf. A. Lionel-Marie, op. cit., pp. 47–48, and unpublished notes by Iliazd, Archives Iliazd.

60. A pseudonym, employed beginning in 1919, formed by contracting "Ilia" and "Zdanevitch." As a matter of fact, everyone in Trigance, a village in the Var district where Iliazd bought an old house, always referred to him as "Monsieur Eli."

61. Conference held on 12 May 1922 at Hubert's, 25 rue de L'Hirondelle, Paris, a locale baptized "L'Université faculté russe" for the occasion.

62. The work is the direct consequence of the preceding work, since Iliazd had asked Giacometti to do his portrait for a frontispiece to *Sentence sans paroles*. Giacometti engraved thirteen sketches directly from life, and, the first having been used as the planned frontispiece, Iliazd had the idea of grouping the twelve others together in another book; however, he offered no explanation with regard to the "celebrated Orbandale" who served to conceal the celebrated "Iliazd"! A. Lionel-Marie, op. cit., p. 77.

63. A bibliographical note found among Iliazd's papers does, however, contain a reference to a certain Orbandale. There is also mention of a work: "Jean Aimes (Aimé) de Chavigna / Le P. Léonard Bertrand / L'illustre Orbandale Chalon 1662."

64. Cf. *La Vie intellectuelle à Toulouse au temps de Godolin*, op. cit., pp. 26–31.

65. Cf. P. Albert-Birot, preface to the posthumous exhibition of works of Roch Grey. Roch Grey died on 3 August 1950. "The enigmatic Roch Grey—this was one of the pseudonyms of the Baroness d'Oettingen, who also signed herself Léonard Pieux—had frequented Apollinaire and participated in 'Soirées de Paris,' and 'Nord-Sud.' She was said to be Serge Férat's sister. She belonged to that Russian colony of artists installed in Paris which Iliazd carefully distinguished from the 'White immigration.'" Cf. F. Chapon, *La Rencontre Iliazd–Picasso*, catalogue for the exhibition at

the Musée d'Art Moderne de la Ville de Paris, 1976.

66. According to Tempel's biography, as established by Iliazd in *L'Art de voir de Guillaume Tempel*, op. cit., "The planet 65 Maximiliana was named by Steinheil in honor of the King of Bavaria, Maximilian II, and later changed to 'Cybele' by German astronomers."

67. Here we should understand "rational" works as those in contrast to the "transrational" works of *zaum*—i.e., phonetic—poetry.

68. Unpublished notes by Iliazd.

69. Marthe Gonneville, "Poésie et typographie," in *Etudes françaises 18/3*, Montreal, Winter 1983, p. 24.

70. Louis Barnier, "Iliazd, notre compagnon . . ." *Bulletin du bibliophile*, Paris, II, 1974. This text is reprinted in *Iliazd*, op. cit. Reference is to this latter publication.

71. Unpublished notes by Iliazd.

72. Quoted in Daniel Payot, *Le Philosophe et l'architect*, Collection philosophie de l'esprit, Editions Aubier/Montaigne, Paris, 1982, p. 92.

73. In May 1917 Iliazd "left St. Petersburg to visit his family and, from there, went on to Turkey, where he took part in an expedition to study medieval architecture. The expedition . . . was organized with subsidies granted by the Historical and Ethnographical Society of the University of Tiflis. . . . Iliazd's contribution was considerable: at least a third of the 150 plans and drawings done are by him." Iliazd's account of the expedition, drawn from his unpublished notes, was as follows: "Having returned to Tiflis at the beginning of the year of the Revolution, I got an offer from M. Takaïchvili to accompany him on an archeological trip into the Turkish areas of Georgia to precede the occupation of those regions by the Russian fighting forces. The purpose of the trip was to visit the five large Georgian churches, all dating from around the tenth and eleventh centuries, well known to historians, but about which little firsthand information existed at the time. Since I had often in earlier years spoken to M. Takaïchvili of my keen desire to visit them, particularly the Church at Parkhal at the foot of Mount Katchkar, the highest peak in the Pontics chain, and to climb that peak, I was overjoyed to receive his offer." Cf. A. Lionel-Marie, op. cit., pp. 50–51.

74. Here Iliazd is alluding to the publication of Scheler's poem and the inverted printing of Picasso's illustration in *Les Lettres françaises*, just as Iliazd was about to issue his own publication.

75. Unpublished notes by Iliazd.

76. Michel Guino, from an interview of 14 January 1978, quoted in A. Lionel-Marie, op. cit., p. 83.

77. Draft of a letter from Iliazd to Max Ernst, 22 January 1961.

78. "Published on the occasion of the exhibition [held] from 29 April to 30 May 1964 at Point Cardinal, 3 rue Jacob, of fine sheets of etchings and writings by Max Ernst to illustrate the data of Wilhelm Tempel brought to light by Iliazd to appear under the title *65 Maximiliana, ou L'Exercice illégal de l'astronomie*."

79. *Le Crève-coeur du vieux soldat* ("The Old Soldier's Heartbreak"),

by Claude Garnier, did not get beyond the planning stage.

80. Iliazd's text on Pirosmanachvili, although not published in French until 1972 in a translation by Andrée Robel and André du Bouchet, had already appeared in 1914 in *Vostok*, a Tiflis newspaper.

81. A Spanish manuscript in the National Library, Madrid. Apparently the National Library at Madrid has two manuscripts of the mendicant friar's text. Iliazd obtained a photocopy of one of them, upon which he partially based his text. It is from that photocopy that we have derived the illustration included here.

82. The words on Iliazd's title page, "Le Frère mendiant, o Libro del conocimiento," refer to the edition established by Marcos Jimenez de la Espada, Madrid, 1877.

83. Excerpt from the Note to the Reader, a text included on the invitation card to the *Exhibition of Pages from "Le Frère mendiant" Illustrated with Drypoints by Pablo Picasso*, Galerie Bignou, May 1959.

84. Cf. Ilia Zdanevitch, *Asel naprakat* ("Dunkey for Rent"), from the anthology *Sofii Georgevne Melnikovoi Fantastitcheskii Kabatcok Tiflis 1917 1918 1919*.

85. Preface to the catalogue of the exhibition *La Rencontre Iliazd–Picasso*, op. cit.

86. Draft of a letter from Iliazd to Matisse, undated, Archives Iliazd.

87. O. Djordjadzé, op. cit., p. 21.

88. Louis Barnier has described this contrast that marked "the two facets of Iliazd's creative genius," cf. "Iliazd, notre compagnon . . ." op. cit., pp. 29–30.

89. Quoted in Marthe Gonneville, op. cit.

90. Cf. Raymond Cogniat, op. cit., p. 4.

91. Statement by Ilia Zdanevitch explaining the poetic principles of The 41st Degree and soliciting followers. The text concludes as follows: "The President of The 41st Degree Section in Paris (France)—Ilia Zdanevitch. Send your address to the central office of The 41st Degree . . . and all the necessary information will be sent you free of charge." Archives Iliazd.

92. Iliazd made the climb in 1917 and completed his account around 1930. This text has never been published. Iliazd published a photograph taken during this expedition in *L'Itinéraire géorgien de Ruy Gonzales de Clavijo et les églises aux confins de Atabégat*, Trigance, 1966. Oddly, there appear to be similarities between the account and the setting and characters described in his novel *Ravissement* ("Rapture"), published in 1930.

93. "The Ascension of Mount Katchkar." Unpublished text, Archives Iliazd.

94. Many pages of Iliazd's narrative make explicit reference to these close relationships between language and geography.

95. Excerpt from *Libro del conocimiento*, narrative of the travels of a fourteenth-century Franciscan, preceded by extracts from *Histoire de la première découverte et conqueste des Canaries faites dès l'an 1402 par . . .*

96. Letter from Iliazd to Mr. Skelton, Director of the Department of Maps, British Museum, London, 6 January 1961. Copy in the Archives Iliazd.

97. "Iliazd to the Reader," reproduced on the invitation card to the *Exhibition of Pages from "Le Frère mendiant*," op. cit.

98. "Had it not been for his love of geography and culture, Iliazd would have been able to get through his entire visit to Berlin and return to Paris without knowing he had been in a German city." Cf. Iliazd, "Berlin et son cabotinage littéraire," Archives Iliazd.

99. M. Riffaterre, op. cit., pp. 125 and 132.

100. Ibid.

101. Gilles Deleuze and Félix Guattari, *Mille Plateaux*, Editions de minuit, Paris, 1980, p. 11.

102. In this connection we might mention Iliazd's interest in Africa because of his marriage with an African princess, Ibironké Akin-semoyin, who died prematurely and by whom he had a son, Chalva. The Yoruba language was one of Iliazd's great interests, evidenced by his preparation of a Yoruba/French dictionary that has attracted the attention of specialists.

PLATES

Before 1920, Iliazd was known as Ilia Zdanevitch; references in the captions that follow vary accordingly. With the exception of the work reproduced in plate 1, Iliazd designed the typography for all of the works reproduced hereafter. Complete information on each plate is given in the Catalogue of the Exhibition.

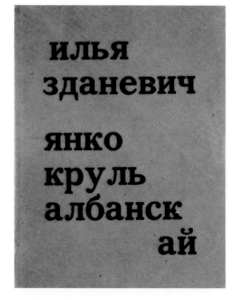

1. Mikhail Larionov. Cover for *Natalia Gontcharova/Mikhail Larionov* by Eli Eganebury (Ilia Zdanevitch). 1913. Lithograph. The New York Public Library, Astor, Lenox, and Tilden Foundations. Spencer Collection. (cat. 7)

2. Ilia Zdanevitch. Cover for *Yanko krul' albanskai* ("Yanko, King of Albania") by Ilia Zdanevitch. May 1918. Typographical composition. Private collection. (cat. 14)

3. Ilia Zdanevitch. Cover for *Rekord niezhnosti* ("Record of Tenderness") by Igor Terentiev. 1919. Typographical composition. Private collection. (cat. 35)

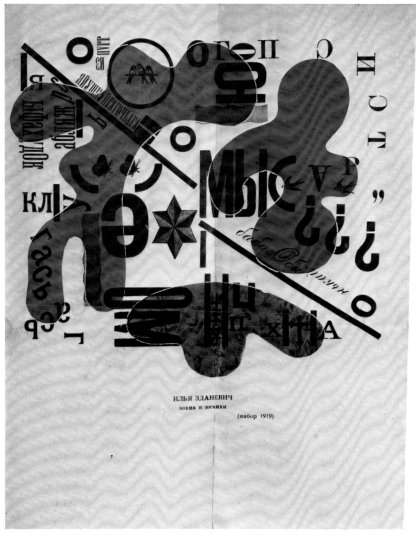

4. Ilia Zdanevitch. Cover for *Ostraf paskhi* ("Easter Eyeland") by Ilia Zdanevitch. 1919. Typographical composition. Private collection. (cat. 15)

5. Ilia Zdanevitch. *Asel naprakat* ("Dunkey for Rent") by Ilia Zdanevitch, from the anthology *Sofii Georgevne Melnikovoi Fantastitcheskii Kabatcok Tiflis 1917 1918 1919* by various authors. September 1919. Typographical composition, printed in color (foldout). Private collection. (cat. 6)

6. Ilia Zdanevitch. *zgA YAkaby* ("As if Zga") by Ilia Zdanevitch. September 7, 1920. Typographical composition (pages interleaved with colored tissue). Private collection. (cat. 16)

7. Nachmann Granovsky. Cover for *lidantYU fAram* ("Ledentu as Beacon") by Iliazd. 1923. Collage. The Museum of Modern Art, New York. Purchase. (cat. 8)

8. Iliazd. *lidantYU fAram* ("Ledentu as Beacon") by Iliazd. 1923. Typographical composition. The Museum of Modern Art, New York. Purchase. (cat. 8)

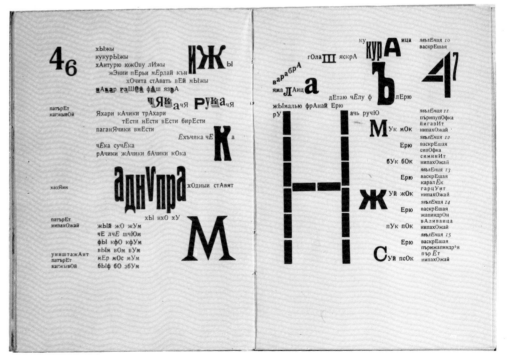

9. Léopold Survage. *Rahel* ("Rachel") by Iliazd. 1941. Woodcut. Calligraphy by Marcel Mée. Private collection. (cat. 29)

10. Pablo Picasso. *Afat* by Iliazd. 1940. Engraving. The Museum of Modern Art, New York. The Louis E. Stern Collection. (cat. 19)

11. Pablo Picasso. *Pismo* ("The Letter") by Iliazd. 1948.
Etching. The Museum of Modern Art, New York. The
Louis E. Stern Collection. (cat. 20)

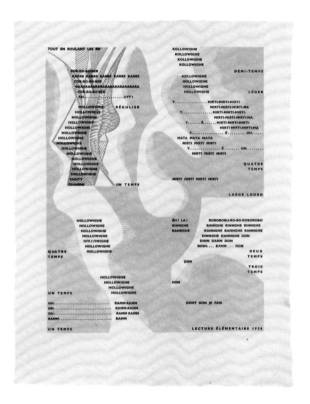

12. Léopold Survage. *Poésie de mots inconnus* by various authors (this text by Michel Seuphor). 1949. Woodcut, printed in color. The Museum of Modern Art, New York. The Louis E. Stern Collection. (cat. 32)

13. Raoul Hausmann. *Poésie de mots inconnus* by various authors (this text by Hausmann). 1949. Woodcut of typographical design. The Museum of Modern Art, New York. The Louis E. Stern Collection. (cat. 32)

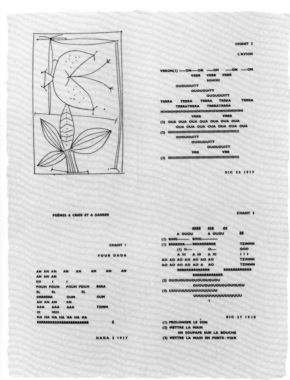

14. Pablo Picasso. *Poésie de mots inconnus* by various authors (this text by Pierre Albert-Birot). 1949. Engraving. The Museum of Modern Art, New York. The Louis E. Stern Collection. (cat. 32)

15. Jean Metzinger. *Poésie de mots inconnus* by various authors (this text by Audiberti). 1949. Drypoint. The Museum of Modern Art, New York. The Louis E. Stern Collection. (cat. 32)

16. Henri Matisse. *Poésie de mots inconnus* by various authors (this text by Ronké Akinsemoyin). 1949. Linoleum cut, printed in color. The Museum of Modern Art, New York. The Louis E. Stern Collection. (cat. 32)

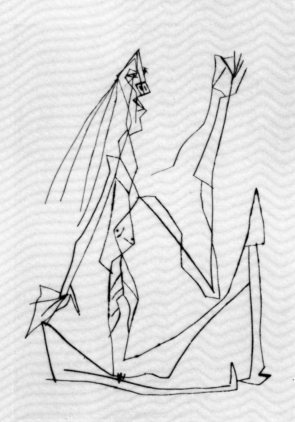

DE SA MEDUSE? SOUBS QUELLE MAUUAISE INFLUENCE ESTES
VOUS NÉE, & POUR QUELLE INCROIABLE PROPRIETÉ ESTES VOUS
DEUENUE ANATOMIE AUANT VOSTRE TRESPAS? N'EST-CE PAS A-
FIN QUE LES MEDECINS VOYANS ALLER LES MOUUEMENS DE VO-
STRE CŒUR, PUISSENT VOIR SI LE BATTEMENT DU POUS VIENT

15

DU SISTOLE, OU DU DIASTOLE? QUANT A MOY IE ME PERDS
PARMY CES CHYMERIQUES PENSÉES, & M'ESTONNE ENCORES D'A-
UANTAGE DE CE QUE VOUS FAICTES LA BELLE, & VOUS VANTEZ
D'VN PUCELAGE QUE LES INCUBES CRAINDROIENT DE CUEILLIR.
SOYEZ BELLE & PUCELLE A LA MAL-HEURE: LES FURIES & LES

16

17. Pablo Picasso. *La Maigre* by Adrian de Monluc (under the name of Guillaume de Vaux). 1952. Drypoint. The Museum of Modern Art, New York. The Louis E. Stern Collection. (cat. 21)

17

PARQUES SEULES PEUUENT DISPUTER DES DEUX AUEC VOUS: NE
CRAIGNEZ PAS QU'AMOUR AUEC SA FLESCHE D'OR PUISSE IA-
MAIS PENETRER VNE POITRINE SI DURE QUE LA VOSTRE; & N'AP-
PREHENDEZ NON PLUS D'ESTRE RAUIE, SI CE N'EST QUE LE VENT
OU LE TOURBILLON VOUS ENLEUE COMME VNE PAILLE OU VN
FESTU, & VOUS TRANSPORTÉ EN QUELQUE REGION INCOGNEUE.
REDOUTEZ SEULEMENT DE TOUS LES MAUX QUI VOUS PEUUENT
ARRIUER, LA CARIE; & DES HOMMES QUI VOUS VERRONT, CEUX
QUI EMMANCHENT DES COUSTEAUX, QUI FONT DES CORNETS
D'ESCRITOIRE, DES DEZ, DES MARQUETERIES, & DES PATENO-
STRES: & N'ESTIMEZ PAS QUE LA MORT VOUS OSE APPROCHER;
CAR VOUS VOYANT SI AFFREUSE, ELLE VOUS PRENDRA POUR SA
SŒUR GERMAINE. TENEZ DONC VN DARD OU VNE FAUX A LA
MAIN, SIMULACRE DE LA FAMINE, ESPRIT DE PERSECUTION, MI-
NISTRE DES VENGEANCES DU CIEL. IE VOUS CONJURE PAR LES
NOMS PLUS GRAUES & PLUS MYSTERIEUX, DE RETOURNER DANS
LES ENFERS.

SUS QU'ON M'APPORTE DE L'EAU BENISTE POUR DISSIPER CE
FANTOSME, IL ME SEMBLE QUE IE LE VOIS, MES CHEUEUX SE

HERISSENT D'HORREUR PENSANT A VN OBJECT SI ESPOUUENTA-
BLE, & LA PLUME TOMBANT DE MA MAIN TRANSIE, & A DEMY
PERCLUSE D'EFFROY & D'ESTONNEMENT M'EMPESCHE DE LUY
DIRE AUTRE CHOSE, SINON, QUE IE LA MAUDITS MILLE & MILLE
FOIS, AUEC SES SOTTES & MENSONGERES VANITEZ DE BEAUTÉ,
& DE PUCELAGE.

18. Pablo Picasso. *La Maigre* by Adrian de Monluc (under the name of Guillaume de Vaux). 1952. Drypoint. The Museum of Modern Art, New York. The Louis E. Stern Collection. (cat. 21)

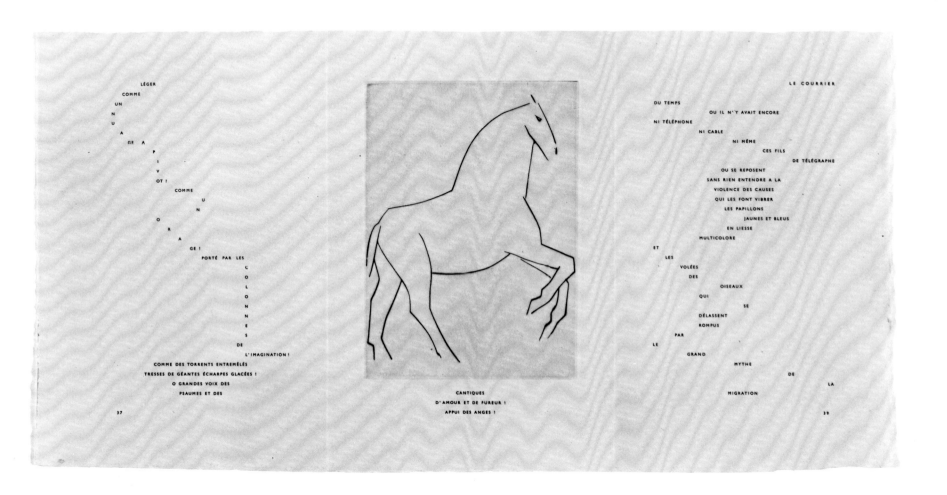

19. Pablo Picasso. *Chevaux de minuit* by Roch Grey (Hélène Baronne d'Oettingen). 1956. Drypoint. The Museum of Modern Art, New York. The Louis E. Stern Collection. (cat. 22)

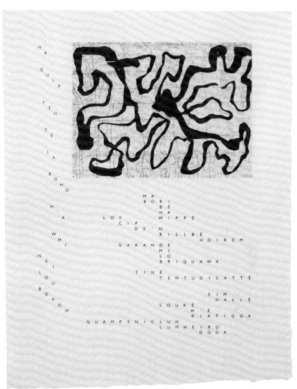

20. Camille Bryen. *Récit du Nord et régions froides pour l'entrée des baillifs de Groenland et Frizland au grand bal de la douairière de Billebahaut* by René Bordier. 1956. Etching and aquatint, printed in color. Private collection. (cat. 3)

21. Raoul Hausmann. *Poèmes et bois* by Raoul Hausmann. 1961. Woodcut, printed in color. Collection Raymond J. Learsy. (cat. 12)

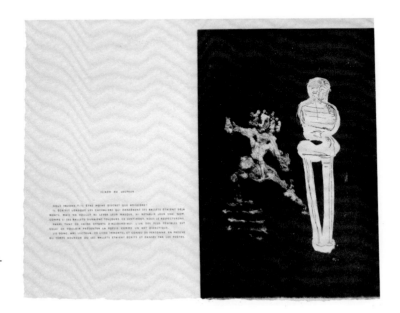

22. Marie-Laure de Noailles. *Traité du balet* by Jehan-François de Boissière. 1953. Etching and aquatint. Private collection. (cat. 18)

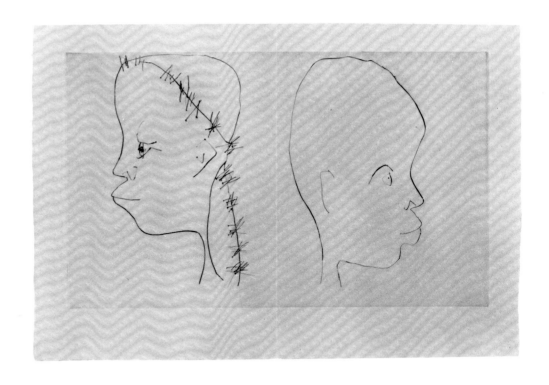

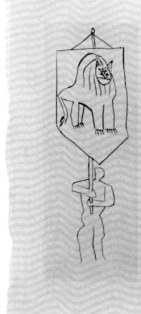

23 and 24. Pablo Picasso. *Le Frère mendiant, o Libro del conocimiento* by Marcos Jimenez de la Espada and Pierre Margry. 1959. Drypoint. Collection Raymond J. Learsy. (cat. 25)

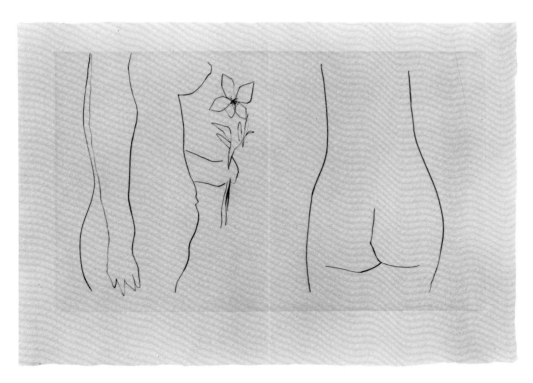

25 and 26. Pablo Picasso. *Le Frère mendiant, o Libro del conocimiento* by
Marcos Jimenez de la Espada and Pierre Margry. 1959. Drypoint.
Collection Raymond J. Learsy. (cat. 25)

27. Pablo Picasso. Portrait of Paul Eluard for *Sillage intangible* by Lucien Scheler. 1958. Drypoint. The Museum of Modern Art, New York. The Louis E. Stern Collection. (cat. 23)

28. Georges Braque. Cover for *Sentence sans paroles* by Iliazd. 1961. Etching on parchment. Private collection. (cat. 1)

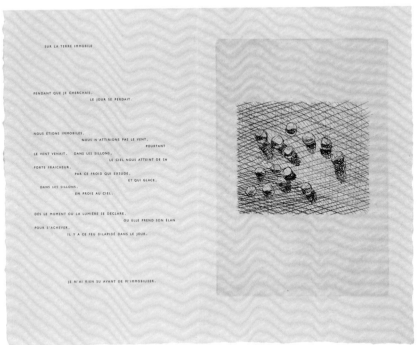

29. Alberto Giacometti. Portrait of Iliazd for *Les Douze Portraits du célèbre Orbandale*. 1962. Etching. The Museum of Modern Art, New York. Purchase. (cat. 5)

30. Jacques Villon. *Ajournement* by André du Bouchet. 1960. Etching executed by Marcel Fiorini after drawing by Villon. The Museum of Modern Art, New York. Gift of Raymond J. Learsy. (cat. 34)

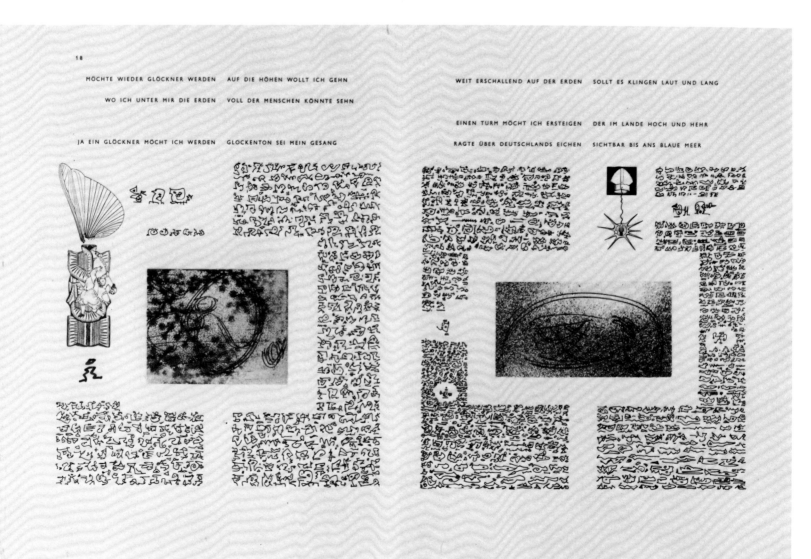

18

MÖCHTE WIEDER GLÖCKNER WERDEN   AUF DIE HÖHEN WOLLT ICH GEHN   WEIT ERSCHALLEND AUF DER ERDEN   SOLLT ES KLINGEN LAUT UND LANG

WO ICH UNTER MIR DIE ERDEN   VOLL DER MENSCHEN KÖNNTE SEHN

EINEN TURM MÖCHT ICH ERSTEIGEN   DER IM LANDE HOCH UND HEHR

JA EIN GLÖCKNER MÖCHT ICH WERDEN   GLOCKENTON SEI MEIN GESANG   RAGTE ÜBER DEUTSCHLANDS EICHEN   SICHTBAR BIS ANS BLAUE MEER

31. Max Ernst. *65 Maximiliana, ou L'Exercice illégal de l'astronomie* by Max Ernst. 1964. Etching and aquatint, printed in color. The New York Public Library, Astor, Lenox, and Tilden Foundations. Spencer Collection, Gift of Dorothea Tanning. (cat. 4)

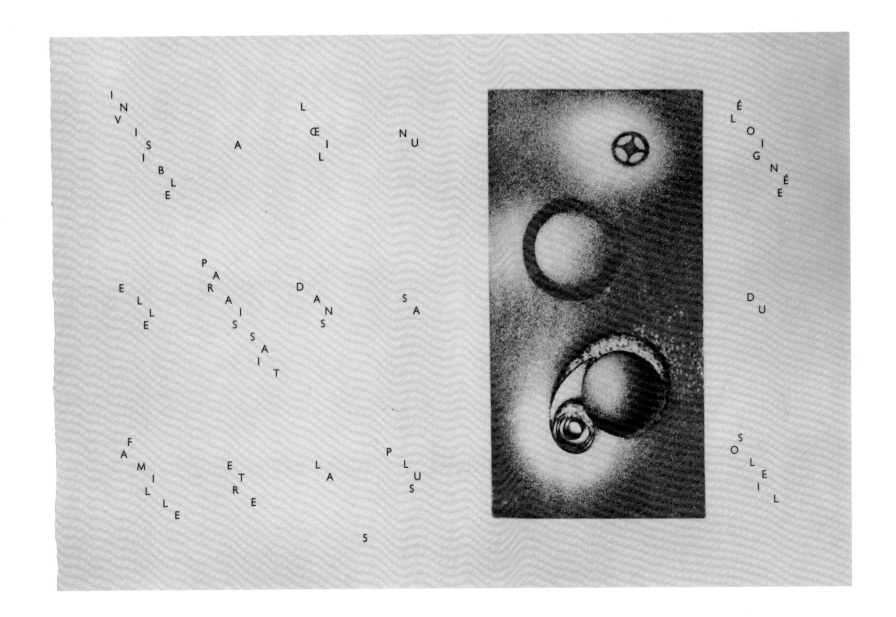

INVISIBLE A L ŒIL NU ÉLOIGNÉE
ELLE PARAISSAIT DANS SA DU
FAMILLE ETRE LA PLUS SOLEIL

5

32. Max Ernst. 65 *Maximiliana, ou L'Exercice illégal de l'astronomie* by Max Ernst. 1964. Etching and aquatint, printed in color. The New York Public Library, Astor, Lenox, and Tilden Foundations. Spencer Collection, Gift of Dorothea Tanning. (cat. 4)

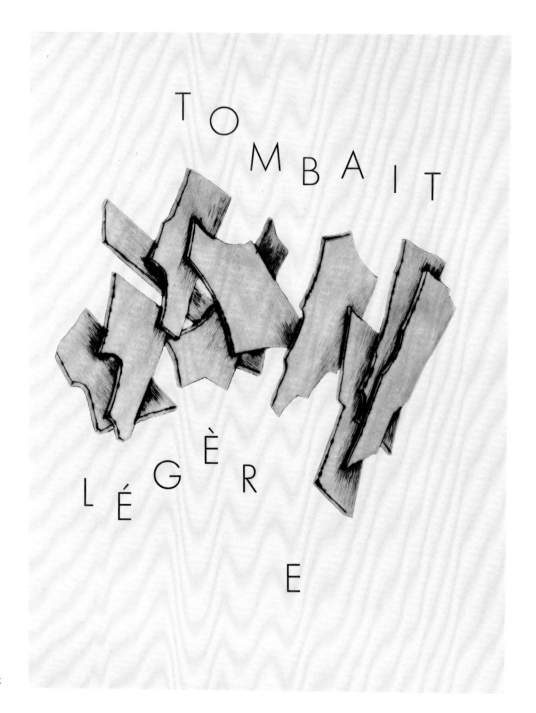

33. Michel Guino. *Un Soupçon* by Paul Eluard. 1965.
Drypoint. The Museum of Modern Art, New York. Gift
of Mme Hélène Iliazd. (cat. 11)

ADRIANDEMONLUC

CUL NOM ED NAIRDA

DEVAVXDECRAMAIL

LIAMARC ED XVAV ED

DE SOLEIL

LIELOS ED

DES CHEVALIERS

SREILAVEHC SED

DE HUIT ANS

SNATIUH ED

DE BASTILLE

ELLITSABED

LE DENTU

UTNED EL

QUAND POURRAI JE

EJ IARRUOP DNAUQ

DÉNICHER CE PAS

SAPEC REHCINED

ENTRE LES DENTS

STNED SEL ERTNE

DE LA MONTAGNE

ENGATNO MALED

DENTELÉE

E ELETNED

34. Iliazd. *Boustrophédon au miroir* by Iliazd. 1971. Typographical composition. Collection Raymond J. Learsy. (cat. 27)

AUX QUATRE COINS DE LA PIÈCE CLOUÉS AUX BOUCHES DE LA LUMIÈRE DU VELUM D'ABOIEMENTS LAVANT LES BRIQUES DU SOLEIL DE LA SUEUR PALE AUBE MORTE DE SOMMEIL TÊTE DU MOUTON EXPIRANT SOUS LA DOUCHE DE SANG DU CLAIRON POSTÉ SOUS LES ROUES DU DRAP DU LIT DÉFAIT LE GRAILLON DU BOUQUET DE ROSES IMITANT SUR LE BOUT DE L'ONGLE LES RIRES ET LES CRIS DE L'ODEUR DU JASMIN ENVELOPPANT LES RAIES BLEU HORTENSIA ET VERT AMANDE LA CHAISE DEBOUT BOUILLANT SUR LE REGARD MITOYEN DU COCORICO DU BOUT D'ÉTOFFE TREMPANT DANS LE CAFÉ LA HACHE DU CARRÉ DE L'ARC EN CIEL DU COSTUME PLEIN DE TROUS DE LA CHANSON COMMENT VEUX TU MON AMOUR MA MAITRESSE MA VIE ROMPRE L'ENNUI ET BRULER LE VOILE DÉCHIRÉ PENDANT AUX CLOUS ROUILLÉS DU TRONC D'ARBRE FONDANT SON BEURRE AU SON DE LA MUSIQUE MILITAIRE QUI PASSE DANS L'ÉGOUT SI LA MAIN LE PIED ET SA BOUCHE ET SES YEUX ET LE COTON QUI FLOTTE DANS L'INTÉRIEUR DU POING FERMÉ DU CRISTAL ET LA CHALEUR ARRIVANT TOUTE GLACÉE DE PEUR DANS LE FEU GROSEILLES TRAINANT LE FILET PLEIN D'ANCHOIS ET LES AIRS DE GUITARE DANS LA BOURRASQUE DES GRAINS DE RIZ NEIGEANT SUR SA JOUE CONDOM DE LUNES ÉVENTAIL D'HUILE D'HIRONDELLES ATTACHANT SA SANDALE DANS L'IMPERCEPTIBLE ODEUR DE PASTÈQUE L'ACQUA VIVA DE SES CHEVEUX MÉLANGÉS ALLUME LA LIE DU SOUFFLE DE LA MAIN QUI AGITE LES AILES DE LA FLUTE

35. Iliazd after Pablo Picasso. *Hommage à Roger Lacourière* by Iliazd and Picasso (this text, "Aux Quatre Coins de la pièce," by Picasso). 1968. Typographical composition after unique proof of Picasso's handwritten engraving. The Museum of Modern Art, New York. Mrs. Stanley Resor Fund (by exchange). (cat. 33)

36. Alberto Magnelli. *Hommage à Roger Lacourière* by Iliazd and Pablo Picasso. 1968. Etching and aquatint. The Museum of Modern Art, New York. Mrs. Stanley Resor Fund (by exchange). (cat. 33)

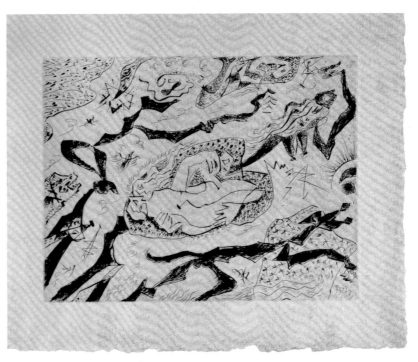

37. André Masson. *Hommage à Roger Lacourière* by Iliazd and Pablo Picasso. 1968. Drypoint and etching. The Museum of Modern Art, New York. Mrs. Stanley Resor Fund (by exchange). (cat. 33)

38. Joan Miró. *Le Courtisan grotesque* by Adrian de Monluc (called Comte de Cramail). 1974. Etching and aquatint, printed in color. The Museum of Modern Art, New York. The Associates Fund. (cat. 17)

INFINITÉ D AUTRES DOUCEURS ᗡᘓ >-ᔕ<ᘜᘓ
LE COURTISAN GROTESQUE NE MANGEA
GUERES PARCE QU IL S ESTOIT FAIT SEIGNER
DE SA VEINE POETIQUE & TIRER SIX ONCES
ᗡᘓ ᔕOYᘓ QUELQUES IOURS AUPARAUANT
MAIS CEPENDANT QUE SA MAISTRESSE
ᗡ ᘓᔕᑌIOꞀꞀᘓ REPAISSOIT COMME VN
COMMISSAIRE IL TENOIT INFINIS DISCOURS DE
POIX ᗡᘓ Ꞁ< ᑌI-ᑎᘓ & CONTOIT <ᑌᘓᑕ
ᗡᘓᔕ Ꞁᘓ⊢⊢Oᑎᔕ LES DIUERS ACCIDENS
DE SON AMOUR & LES TRAUAUX SANS TRAUAIL
ᗡᑌ ᔕ-ᘓᑌᖇ ᗡ<ᑌ-⊢ & COUUROIT
DU VOILE ᗡᘓ Ꞁ< ᑎᑌ-⊢ AUEC PLUSIEURS
FIGURES ᗡᘓ Ꞁ<ᖇᘓ⊢-ᑎ & ARTIFICES
< ᖴᘓᑌ LES BONNES ADUENTURES QUI LUY
ESTOIENT ESCHEUES ᑭ<ᖇ ᗡᘓᔕᔕᑌᔕ
ᔕᘓᔕ ᘜ<ᘜᘓᔕ APRES MAINTS DIALOGUES
ᗡ ᘓᖇ<ᔕᘔᘓ ILS SE SEPARERENT BONS 7

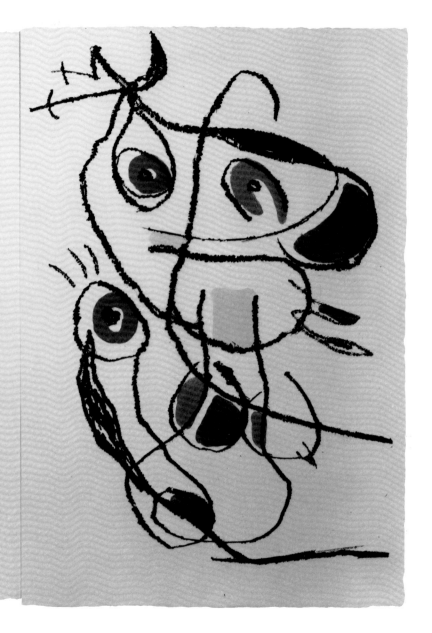

39. Joan Miró. *Le Courtisan grotesque* by Adrian de Monluc (called Comte de Cramail). 1974. Etching and aquatint, printed in color.
The Museum of Modern Art, New York. The Associates Fund. (cat. 17)

Iliazd as "The Triumph of Cubism," at the "Bal banal," March 14, 1924

CHRONOLOGY

The following chronology is based on those written by Françoise Woimant, Annick Lionel-Marie, and Hélène Iliazd with Régis Gayraud (see Selected Bibliography), and is limited to Iliazd's major activities and interests vis-à-vis his development as a publisher and poet.

1894 April 21, born Ilia Zdanevitch in Tiflis, Georgia, to Mikhail Zdanevitch and Valentina Gamgeklidze. Shows talent at an early age for art, music, geography, and mathematics. His brother, Kiril, two years his senior, will become an artist.

1911 The Zdanevitch family lodges the painter Boris Lopatinski, who brings from Paris Marinetti's first Futurist manifestos. Ilia learns them by heart, later writing, "For me, admirer of the Symbolists, it was a conversion."

Moves to St. Petersburg to study law. There meets painters Victor Barthe and Mikhail Ledentu, who introduce him in avant-garde circles.

1912 January, presents Futurist manifesto at Trotsky Theater during meeting organized by the Union of Youth, of which poet Alexei Kruchenykh and painters David and Nikolai Burliuk, Mikhail Larionov, and Natalia Gontcharova are members. Begins to emerge as key figure in Russian Futurism.

Summer, discovers naïve paintings of Georgian artist Niko Pirosmanachvili while vacationing in Tiflis with Kiril and Ledentu. "The painting, painted on the black waxed cloth with which cabaret owners covered their tables, was astonishingly compatible with our artistic convictions due to its pictorial characteristics," Kiril later writes.

1913 Winter, meets Pirosmanachvili, called Pirosmani, in Tiflis and commissions portrait. Publishes an article on him in local newspaper.

Spring, at age nineteen publishes his first book, under the pseudonym Eli Eganebury: *Natalia Gontcharova/Mikhail Larionov*, a study and catalogue raisonné of their painting.

Declares at Polytechnical Museum in Moscow: "An American shoe is more beautiful than the Venus de Milo."

November, gives conference with Ledentu in Moscow on "everythingism" (*vsechestvo*), which aspires to "use and combine all the forms of art known in the past," in reaction to the fanatic narrow-mindedness of certain Futurists.

December, with Larionov writes the proclamation "Why We Paint Our Faces," published in the magazine *Argus*: "We have tied art to life. . . . The synthesis of decoration and illustration is the basis of our painting . . . and that is why we paint ourselves." (With Gontcharova they had painted signs and numbers on their faces symbolizing the union of man and building.)

1914 January 27–28, Marinetti holds conference in Moscow and is welcomed by Ilia, who presents the latest Futurist manifesto. Ilia refuses, however, to sign manifesto against Italian Futurism circulated by Marinetti the next day.

Signs pact of Centrifuge movement. Writes another article on Pirosmanachvili for Tiflis newspaper, to be reprinted in his *Pirosmanachvili 1914*, 1972.

August, Germany, Russia, and Austria declare war. Ledentu and Kiril are drafted.

Ilia Zdanevitch, c. 1911

Portrait of Ilia by Niko Pirosmanachvili, 1913

"Why We Paint Our Faces," *Argus*, December 1913

Ilia frequently travels to the Caucasus as war correspondent for St. Petersburg newspaper. Continues legal studies.

1917   February, renounces law profession after receiving degree and official post.

July–August, goes on archeological expedition in Turkey, after which he makes solo ascent of Kaçkar Daği, highest mountain in Pontics chain. Names anonymous peak in memory of Ledentu, who was killed in the war.

October, returns to Tiflis after October Revolution and becomes apprentice at Caucasian printing association.

November, with Kruchenykh, Igor Terentiev, and Kiril founds University of The 41st Degree, dedicated to the advancement of avant-garde poetry.

1918   Publishes first of five *dras* (one-act folk plays) in *Aslaablitchia* ("Dunkeyness") cycle: *Yanko krul' albanskai* ("Yanko, King of Albania"), written in 1916 in *zaum*, a "transrational," asyntactical language in which meanings derive purely from words' sounds. The typographical design by Ilia is conceived for both silent reading and recitation.

1919   Begins publishing books under The 41st Degree imprint. His second and third *dras, Asel naprakat* ("Dunkey for Rent"; written 1918) and *Ostraf paskhi* ("Easter Eyeland"), are the first issued.

1920   September, publishes fourth *dra, zgA YAkaby* ("As if Zga"), under the name Iliazd, first published use of the contraction he will favor henceforth.

1921   Late November, moves to Paris. Lives with Larionov initially, meeting fellow Russian émigrés as well as Picasso, Robert Delaunay, and the Dadaists, to whom he is instantly attracted. Installs University of The 41st Degree in the Montparnasse café Le Caméléon and begins series of conferences, despite disappointment with artistic life in Paris.

1922   Works for Sonia Delaunay in fabric design. Holds conferences on *zaum* poetry. Becomes friendly with Dadaist Tristan Tzara and Surrealist Paul Eluard.

Named secretary of union of Russian artists, whose main activity is the organization of balls and fêtes. "Bal transmental" of 1923 and "Bal banal" of 1924 will be noted successes.

November, organizes evening in honor of Russian avant-garde poet Vladimir Mayakovsky. After dinner Iliazd and Serge Romoff create *Tcherez* group with other Russian artists interested in experimental theater. Their soirées will attract writers Pierre Reverdy, Antonin Artaud, and Max Jacob.

Iliazd, 1922

Letter from Marinetti to Iliazd, 1922

December, goes to Berlin to meet Mayakovsky and other Russian artists living there. Later writes an account of the trip entitled "Berlin and Its Literary Fraud."

1923 July 6, organizes "La Soirée du *Coeur à barbe*" in honor of Tzara and his play *Le Coeur à gaz*. General brawl that breaks out at evening's close over a disagreement between Tzara and Eluard marks the end of Dada and *Tcherez*. Eluard reneges on promise to write preface for Iliazd's final *dra*, dedicated to Ledentu.

Fall, *lidantYU fAram* ("Ledentu as Beacon"), the culmination of Iliazd's *zaum* writing, is published. This fifth and last *dra* is printed at L'Imprimerie Union, where all Iliazd's subsequent books will be printed.

1924 Lives for a while with Max Ernst and Gala Eluard in Eaubonne.

October, France officially recognizes U.S.S.R. Friends in Russian delegation offer Iliazd post as interpreter.

1925 Participates in Surrealist meetings at place Blanche.

June, exhibits *lidantYU fAram* and other 41st Degree publications in Russian pavilion at World's Fair.

Believing "Futurism is still the official art but not for long; in 1926 it will be banned," Iliazd renounces further activity in Russian literary circles, participating only in union balls.

1926 Marries Simone Axel Brocard, with whom he will have two children. Loses post at embassy and returns to fabric design.

1927 Begins working for Coco Chanel in fabric design, a position he will hold until 1933.

1928–37 Period of economic hardship. Continues writing poetry and fiction. Pursues research in architecture of Georgian and Armenian churches.

1938 Divorces and moves to rue Mazarine in Picasso's neighborhood. They frequently take meals together in local restaurants.

1940 Publishes first *de luxe* book, *Afat*, seventy-six of his own classic Russian sonnets, with illustrations by Picasso. Iliazd writes of the publication: "Who would have foreseen that . . . Iliazd, eternal clown . . . would become the most austere representative of sorrowful and classical poetry?"

1941 Publishes *Rahel* ("Rachel"), two of his own sonnets in Russian on the theme of war, ornamented by Léopold Survage. Edition includes French translation of Iliazd's text by Eluard.

1942 Marries the Nigerian princess Ibironké Akinsemoyin, with whom he will have a son. His research focuses on Africa and Benin culture.

1945 Works in high-fashion jersey design with François Victor-Hugo. Second wife dies.

1946 Frequently travels to south of France, where he reencounters Picasso and becomes interested in ceramics.

His conference "Vingt Ans de futurisme" provokes violent reaction from new "letterist" movement. Of it Iliazd writes: "In Paris, the year 1946 was marked by the appearance of [the letterist] Isidore Isou. . . . Isou passed off his imitations of the phonetic poets from the 1920s and *zaum* poetry as a new form of poetry baptized by him 'letterist.'"

1947 In response to letterists, gives another conference, "Après Nous le lettrisme," which degenerates into fisticuffs.

1948 Writes and publishes third *de luxe* book, *Pismo* ("The Letter"), with illustrations by Picasso.

1949 Edits and publishes *Poésie de mots inconnus*, an anthology of phonetic and *zaum* poetry written between 1912 and 1932, with illustrations by twenty-three different artists. Holds press conference "to demonstrate the anteriority of Futurist and Dada investigations" with regard to letterism.

Writes a "ballet in words," *La Chasse sous-marine*, in French *zaum*. Commissions sets from Matisse, but work is never staged.

1952 Publishes *La Maigre*, a seventeenth-century tale by Adrian de Monluc, with illustrations by Picasso. Uses exclusively capital letters set in the neutral Gill typeface, with varied spacing between, "a revolution in typography," according to Louis Barnier, his printer.

1953 Publishes *Traité du ballet* by Jehan-François de Boissière, Monluc's secretary, with illustrations by Marie-Laure de Noailles. It is dedicated to the glory of ballet in Toulouse under Louis XIII, during "the happy era when ballets were written and danced by poets."

1954–55 Upon Marcel Duchamp's request, designs a revised version of the container for Duchamp's *La Boîte en valise*.

Discovers the early-seventeenth-century poem *Le Crève-coeur du vieux soldat*. Picasso promises illustrations but repeatedly postpones work on commission.

1956 Publishes *Récit du Nord et régions froides pour l'entrée des baillifs de Groenland et Frizland au grand bal de la douairière de Billebahaut* by René Bordier, another contemporaneous treatment

Poster for "La Soirée du *Coeur à barbe*," 1923, designed by Iliazd

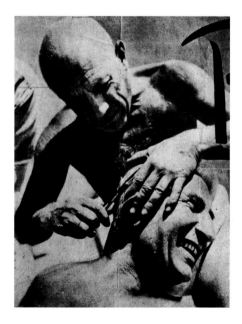

Iliazd and Picasso, Golfe Juan, 1947

of seventeenth-century ballet in Louis XIII's court. Contains a totally phonetic passage in *zaum*-like consonants. Illustrated by Camille Bryen.

Publishes epic poem *Chevaux de minuit* by Roch Grey, with illustrations by Picasso. It is Iliazd's homage to the obscure, multifaceted author, who wrote and painted under various pseudonyms.

1958   July, publishes *Sillage intangible*, Lucien Scheler's poem in memory of Eluard, for which Picasso executes a portrait. It is printed on "the most beautiful japan paper one could find in Paris, that which the publisher Pelletan acquired in 1906 from Bing, exporter of items from China and Japan."

1959   Publishes *Le Frère mendiant, o Libro del conocimiento*, illustrated by Picasso. This tale of the fourteenth-century voyages of an anonymous Franciscan monk appealed to Iliazd's strong interests in exploratory expeditions and Africa.

1960   Publishes *Ajournement*, poetry by André du Bouchet, illustrated by Jacques Villon.

1961   April, publishes *Poèmes et bois*, written and illustrated by Raoul Hausmann, Dadaist pioneer of phonetic and visual poetry.

December, publishes *Sentence sans paroles*, Russian poems by Iliazd written in the form of a "garland of sonnets," in which fourteen sonnets are joined, as each begins with the last verse of the preceding one, and a fifteenth sonnet reunites the last verses of each of the fourteen. Cover by Georges Braque and frontispiece portrait of Iliazd by Alberto Giacometti.

1962   Publishes *Les Douze Portraits du célèbre Orbandale*, a book without text comprised of twelve portraits of Iliazd by Giacometti, who had etched thirteen plates in response to Iliazd's request for a portrait for *Sentence sans paroles*. The "famous Orbandale" is none other than Iliazd.

1964   Publishes *65 Maximiliana, ou L'Exercice illégal de l'astronomie*, with text and illustrations by Ernst, recounting the life of Ernst Wilhelm Tempel, scorned German astronomer who discovered the planet 65 Maximiliana.

1965   Publishes *Un Soupçon* by Eluard, illustrated by the sculptor Michel Guino. This poem had been offered to Iliazd by Eluard in a spirit of reconciliation after the "Soirée du *Coeur à barbe*" incident.

1966   Has difficult correspondence with Vladimir Markov, who is researching his *Russian Futurism: A History*. Iliazd refuses to speak of the past.

1967   Winter, Kiril, whom Iliazd has not seen since 1921, obtains visa and travels to France.

Writes text in homage to the printer Roger Lacourière for print review *Nouvelles de l'estampe*.

1968   Marries ceramicist Hélène Douard.

Publishes *Hommage à Roger Lacourière*, in which texts by Iliazd and Picasso are illustrated with previously unpublished prints by thirteen different artists who worked with the renowned printer at his Montmartre atelier.

1969   Exhibition of Pirosmanachvili's paintings at Musée des Arts décoratifs in Paris. Iliazd rediscovers in show more than sixty works once belonging to him. Kiril completes a biography of the artist shortly before he dies in November in Tiflis.

1971   Writes and publishes *Boustrophédon au miroir*, illustrated by Georges Ribemont-Dessaignes. Iliazd was inspired by inscriptions in this form on ancient Greek stelae and vases. The reading from right to left recalls *zaum* poetry.

1972   December, publishes *Pirosmanachvili 1914*, with a portrait of the artist by Picasso.

1974   Publishes *Le Courtisan grotesque*, a satire by Monluc, illustrated by Joan Miró. Iliazd illuminates author's enigmatic use of words with double meanings, italicized in a 1630 edition, by shifting their typographical orientation. Iliazd and Miró had collaborated on the project for twenty years.

Celebrates his eightieth birthday. Sonia Delaunay, Max Ernst, Joan Miró, Louis Barnier, Camille Bryen, André du Bouchet, Georges Ribemont-Dessaignes, Lucien Scheler, Georges Ramié, Madeleine Lacourière, Jacques Frélaut, Françoise Woimant, and François Chapon contribute pieces for *Bulletin du bibliophile* special issue on Iliazd.

1975   Iliazd dies suddenly on Christmas Day.

SELECTED BIBLIOGRAPHY

BOOKS AND CATALOGUES

Compton, Susan P. *The World Backwards: Russian Futurist Books 1912–16*. London: British Museum Publications Ltd., 1978.

Garvey, Eleanor M. *The Artist and the Book: 1860–1960* (exhibition catalogue). Boston: Museum of Fine Arts; Cambridge, Mass.: Harvard College Library, 1961. Second edition 1972.

de Ginestet, Colette, and Catherine Pouillon. *Jacques Villon: Les Estampes et les illustrations, Catalogue raisonné*. Paris: Arts et Métiers Graphiques, 1979.

Goeppert, Sebastian, Herma Goeppert-Frank, and Patrick Cramer. *Pablo Picasso, The Illustrated Books: Catalogue Raisonné*. Geneva: Patrick Cramer, Publisher, 1983.

Greet, Anne Hyde. "Max Ernst and the Artist's Book: From *Fiat Modes* to *Maximiliana*," in Robert Rainwater, ed., *Max Ernst: Beyond Surrealism* (exhibition catalogue). New York: The New York Public Library; Oxford and New York: Oxford University Press, 1986.

Iliazd, Hélène, with Régis Gayraud. *Iliazd 1894–1975*. Chronology published on the occasion of the exhibition *Iliazd, Maître d'oeuvre du livre moderne*. Montreal: L'Université du Québec à Montréal, 1984.

Janecek, Gerald. *The Look of Russian Literature: Avant-Garde Visual Experiments, 1900–1930*. Princeton: Princeton University Press, 1984.

Leppien, Helmut. *Max Ernst: Das graphische Werk*. Houston: Menil Foundation; Cologne: Verlag M. DuMont Schauberg, 1975.

Lust, Herbert C. *Giacometti: The Complete Graphics*. New York: Tudor Publishing, 1970.

Markov, Vladimir. *Russian Futurism: A History*. Berkeley and Los Angeles: University of California Press, 1968.

Montreal, L'Université du Québec à Montréal. *Iliazd, Maître d'oeuvre du livre moderne* (exhibition catalogue), 1984.

Paris, Centre Georges Pompidou, Musée National d'Art Moderne. *Iliazd* (exhibition catalogue), 1978. Chronology by Annick Lionel-Marie.

Paris, Musée d'Art Moderne de la Ville de Paris. *La Rencontre Iliazd–Picasso: Hommage à Iliazd* (exhibition catalogue), 1976. Chronology by Françoise Woimant.

Vallier, Dora. *Braque: L'Oeuvre gravé, Catalogue raisonné*. Lausanne: Flammarion, 1982.

ARTICLES

Chapon, François, ed. "Hommage à Iliazd," *Bulletin du bibliophile* (Paris), II (1974). Special issue on Iliazd. Contributors: Sonia Delaunay, Max Ernst, Joan Miró, Louis Barnier, Camille Bryen, André du Bouchet, Georges Ribemont-Dessaignes, Lucien Scheler, Georges Ramié, Madeleine Lacourière, Jacques Frélaut, and Françoise Woimant.

Germain, André. "Ilia Zdanevitch et le surdadaïsme russe," *Créer* (Liège), vol. 2, no. 1 (January–February 1923).

Woimant, Françoise, and Marcelle Elgrishi. "Iliazd, Tériade et Pierre Lecuire, trois grands éditeurs de notre temps," *Nouvelles de l'estampe* (Paris), no. 15 (May–June 1974).

Woimant, Françoise, et al. "Iliazd," *Nouvelles de l'estampe* (Paris), no. 26 (March–April 1976).

CATALOGUE OF THE EXHIBITION

The two sections of the catalogue, *Illustrated Books* and *Drawings, Posters, and Announcements*, are organized alphabetically by artist, with each artist's works listed chronologically. The purely typographical works Iliazd designed are listed under his name.

Before 1920, Iliazd was known as Ilia Zdanevitch; citations in the entries that follow vary accordingly.

ILLUSTRATED BOOKS

All publications of The 41st Degree were designed by Iliazd, who began issuing books under the imprint in 1919. Page dimensions are given in inches and centimeters, height preceding width. Dates and places of publication enclosed in parentheses do not appear on the works. Some books are exhibited with preparatory material, the lenders of which are acknowledged by the following symbols: † Private collection; †† Bibliothèque Nationale, Paris; ††† Marie Bertin, Paris. Not mentioned below but included in the exhibition are duplicate pages and covers, and documentary material not of a preparatory nature.

Braque, Georges, and   French, 1882–1963
Alberto Giacometti   Swiss, 1901–1966

1. *Sentence sans paroles* by Iliazd. Paris, Le Degré Quarante et Un, 1961. Etching (on cover) by Braque and etching by Giacometti, 7⅛ × 4⅞" (18.1 × 12.4 cm). Private collection. *See plate 28.* Preparatory material: original drawing by Braque for cover, maquette †.
2. *Sentence sans paroles.* Second copy with special binding by Henri Mercher. Collection Raymond J. Learsy.

Bryen, Camille   French, 1907–1976

3. *Récit du Nord et régions froides pour l'entrée des baillifs de Groenland et Frizland au grand bal de la douairière de Billebahaut* by René Bordier. Paris, pour la cause du Degré Quarante et Un, 1956. Etching and aquatint, printed in color, 17⁵⁄₁₆ × 13³⁄₁₆" (44 × 33.5 cm). Private collection. *See plate 20.*

Ernst, Max   French, Born Germany, 1891–1976

4. *65 Maximiliana, ou L'Exercice illégal de l'astronomie* by Max Ernst. (Paris,) Le Degré Quarante et Un, 1964. Thirty-four etchings and aquatints, printed in color, 16¹⁄₁₆ × 24" (40.8 × 61 cm). *See plates 31 and 32.* Accompanied by the related booklet *L'Art de voir de Guillaume Tempel* by Iliazd. Paris, Iliazd, 1964. Etching and aquatint, printed in color, 12⅜ × 4⅛" (31.5 × 10.5 cm). The New York Public Library, Astor, Lenox, and Tilden Foundations. Spencer Collection, Gift of Dorothea Tanning. Preparatory material: copperplates, typographical and layout studies †; miniature maquette with pictograms (color memory aids), booklet of various proofs of etchings, two zinc plates for text and corresponding proofs, typographical maquettes and corresponding proofs, annotated typographical maquettes ††.

Giacometti, Alberto

5. *Les Douze Portraits du célèbre Orbandale.* (Paris,) À l'éditeur qui ne fait pas aciérer les planches de cuivre (Iliazd), 1962. Twelve etchings, 13 × 6¾" (33 × 17.1 cm) (variable). The Museum of Modern Art, New York. Purchase. *See plate 29.*

Gontcharova, Natalia   Russian, 1881–1962

6. *Asel naprakat* ("Dunkey for Rent") by Ilia Zdanevitch, from the anthology *Sofii Georgevne Melnikovoi Fantastitcheskii Kabatcok Tiflis 1917 1918 1919* by various authors. Tiflis, The 41st Degree, September 1919. Five collages of reproductions of drawings by Gontcharova, 7¹⁄₁₆ × 5⁵⁄₁₆" (18 × 13.5 cm). Private collection. *See plate 5.*

Gontcharova, Natalia, and
Mikhail Larionov   Russian, 1881–1964

7. *Natalia Gontcharova/Mikhail Larionov* by Eli Eganebury (Ilia Zdanevitch). Moscow, Editions Tz. A. Munster, 1913. Eight lithographs (four by each artist), 11¼ × 8⅝" (28.5 × 21.9 cm). The New York Public Library, Astor, Lenox, and Tilden Foundations. Spencer Collection. See *plate 1*.

Granovsky, Nachmann   Russian, Born 1898

8. *lidantYU fAram* ("Ledentu as Beacon") by Iliazd. Paris, éditions du 41°, 1923. Collage (on cover), 7½ × 5½" (19 × 14 cm). The Museum of Modern Art, New York. Purchase. See *plates 7 and 8*.

9. *lidantYU fAram*. Second copy. Collection Raymond J. Learsy.

10. *lidantYU fAram*. Third copy. The New York Public Library, Astor, Lenox, and Tilden Foundations. Spencer Collection.

Guino, Michel   French, Born 1926

11. *Un Soupçon* by Paul Eluard. Paris, Le Degré Quarante et Un, 1965. Sixteen drypoints (including cover), printed in color and in black, 16⁹/₁₆ × 12" (42 × 30.5 cm). The Museum of Modern Art, New York. Gift of Mme Hélène Iliazd. See *plate 33*. Preparatory material: studies for typographical layout and placement of illustrations, copperplates †.

Hausmann, Raoul   Austrian, 1886–1971

12. *Poèmes et bois* by Raoul Hausmann. Paris, Degré Quarante et Un, 1961. Five woodcuts, printed in color, 16¼ × 12½" (41.2 × 30.8 cm). Collection Raymond J. Learsy. See *plate 21*. Preparatory material: woodblocks †; proofs of woodcuts, printed in gouache, two double-page proofs of text and illustrations, printed on graph paper ††.

13. *Poèmes et bois*. Second copy. Private collection.

Iliazd (Ilia Zdanevitch)   Russian, 1894–1975. To France 1921

14. *Yanko krul' albanskai* ("Yanko, King of Albania") by Ilia Zdanevitch. Tiflis, Syndicate, May 1918. Typography, 5¾ × 4½" (14.5 × 11.5 cm). Private collection. See *plate 2*.

15. *Ostraf paskhi* ("Easter Eyeland") by Ilia Zdanevitch. Tiflis, Typography of the Union of Georgian Cities, 1919. Typography, 8½ × 6⅞" (21.5 × 17.5 cm). Private collection. See *plate 4*.

16. *zgA YAkaby* ("As if Zga") by Ilia Zdanevitch. Tiflis, The 41st Degree, September 7, 1920. Typography (pages interleaved with colored tissue), 6½ × 4½" (16.5 × 11.5 cm). Private collection. See *plate 6*.

Miró, Joan   Spanish, 1893–1983

17. *Le Courtisan grotesque* by Adrian de Monluc (called Comte de Cramail). (Paris,) Le Degré Quarante et Un, 1974. Twenty-three etchings with aquatint and drypoint (including cover), printed in color, 16½ × 11½" (41.9 × 29.2 cm) (variable).

The Museum of Modern Art, New York. The Associates Fund. See *plates 38 and 39*. Preparatory material: two copperplates for cover, two reduced maquettes, typographical studies, proofs of etchings, printed in black on china paper †; 1960 maquette (oblong, narrow format), proofs of illustrations, printed in black with annotated text, typographical maquette with slanted letters ††.

de Noailles, Marie-Laure   French, 1902–1970

18. *Traité du balet* by Jehan-François de Boissière. (Paris,) Le Degré Quarante et Un, 1953. Sixty-six etchings, some with aquatint, 14⁹/₁₆ × 10⅝" (37 × 27 cm). Private collection. See *plate 22*.

Picasso, Pablo   Spanish, 1881–1973. To France 1904

19. *Afat* by Iliazd. (Paris,) Le Degré Quarante et Un, 1940. Four engravings and two aquatints, 8 × 11⅞" (20.3 × 30.2 cm) (variable). The Museum of Modern Art, New York. The Louis E. Stern Collection. See *plate 10*.

20. *Pismo* ("The Letter") by Iliazd. (Paris,) Latitud Cuarenta y Uno, 1948. Five etchings (including cover) and two drypoints, 14¼ × 3⁷/₁₆–9⅝" (36.2 × 8.8–24.5 cm) (folded variable widths). The Museum of Modern Art, New York. The Louis E. Stern Collection. See *plate 11*. Preparatory material: proofs of cover etching on parchment †.

21. *La Maigre* by Adrian de Monluc (under the name of Guillaume de Vaux). (Paris,) Le Degré Quarante et Un (1952). Ten drypoints (including cover), 16¼ × 9⅛" (41.3 × 23.2 cm) (variable). The Museum of Modern Art, New York. The Louis E. Stern Collection. See *plates 17 and 18*. Preparatory material: set of corrected typographical proofs in oblong format, proof of drypoint on cover ††.

22. *Chevaux de minuit* by Roch Grey (Hélène Baronne d'Oettingen). Cannes and Paris, Aux bons soins du Degré Quarante et Un, 1956. One drypoint (on cover) and twelve drypoints and engravings, 12⅛ × 8¼" (30.7 × 21 cm) (variable). The Museum of Modern Art, New York. The Louis E. Stern Collection. See *plate 19*. Preparatory material: cancelled copperplates, one signed proof of engraving without typography †.

23. *Sillage intangible* by Lucien Scheler. (Paris,) Le Degré Quarante et Un, 1958. Drypoint, 9¹/₁₆–9¼ × 10–11¹¹/₁₆" (23–23.5 × 25.4–29.7 cm) (folded variable widths). The Museum of Modern Art, New York. The Louis E. Stern Collection. See *plate 27*.

24. *Le Frère mendiant, o Libro del conocimiento* by Marcos Jimenez de la Espada and Pierre Margry. (Paris,) Latitud Cuarenta y Uno, 1959. Sixteen drypoints (including cover), 16⅝ × 13½" (42.2 × 34.4 cm). Example of book with cancelled plates. Private collection. Preparatory material: copperplates, three proofs of drypoints, photostats of original nineteenth-century text †; printing instruction chart, maquette for typographical layout and placement of illustrations ††.

25. *Le Frère mendiant, o Libro del conocimiento*. Second, unique example of book with impressions of each drypoint on china, imperial japan, and ancient japan papers, special binding by Henri Mercher; 16¼–17¹⁵⁄₁₆ × 11¾–12¾" (41.3–45.6 × 29.8–32.4 cm) (variable according to paper). Collection Raymond J. Learsy. *See plates 23–26.*
26. *Pirosmanachvili 1914* by Iliazd. (Paris,) Le Degré Quarante et Un, 1972. Drypoint, 12⅛ × 7¼" (30.8 × 18.4 cm) (variable). The Museum of Modern Art, New York. Mrs. Stanley Resor Fund (by exchange). *See figs. 1 and 2, Isselbacher.*

Ribemont-Dessaignes, Georges   **French, 1884–1974**

27. *Boustrophédon au miroir* by Iliazd. Paris, Le Degré Quarante et Un, 1971. Eleven etchings (including cover), 9¾ × 6½" (24.8 × 16.5 cm). Collection Raymond J. Learsy. *See plate 34.*
28. *Boustrophédon au miroir*. Second copy. Private collection.

Survage, Léopold   **Russian, 1879–1968. To France 1908**

29. *Rahel* ("Rachel") by Iliazd. Paris, Imprimerie Union, 1941. Two woodcuts, 23⅝ × 16⅛" (60 × 41 cm). Calligraphy by Marcel Mée. Private collection. *See plate 9.* Preparatory material: ink wash drawing by Survage †††.

Various Artists

30. *Poésie de mots inconnus* by various authors. (Paris,) Le Degré 41, 1949. Ten etchings, six lithographs, seven woodcuts, two engravings, one linoleum cut, and one line cut, printed in black and in color, 6½ × 5¼" (16.5 × 13.3 cm) (sheets folded in quarto). Collection Raymond J. Learsy. Artists: Jean Arp, Georges Braque, Camille Bryen, Marc Chagall, Oscar Dominguez, Serge Férat, Alberto Giacometti, Albert Gleizes, Raoul Hausmann, Henri Laurens, Fernand Léger, Alberto Magnelli, André Masson, Henri Matisse, Jean Metzinger, Joan Miró, Pablo Picasso, Georges Ribemont-Dessaignes, Léopold Survage, after Sophie Taeuber-Arp, Edgard Tytgat, Jacques Villon, Wols (born Alfred Wolfgang Schültze).
31. *Poésie de mots inconnus*. Second copy. Private collection.
32. *Poésie de mots inconnus*. Third copy. 12¾ × 10" (32.3 × 25.4 cm) (variable, sheets not folded). The Museum of Modern Art, New York. The Louis E. Stern Collection. *See plates 12–16.*
33. *Hommage à Roger Lacourière* by Iliazd and Pablo Picasso. (Paris,) Le Degré Quarante et Un, 1968. Five etchings, four etchings with drypoint, two etchings with aquatint, one aquatint, and one drypoint, printed in black and in color; 9⅛ × 11½" (23.2 × 29.2 cm). The Museum of Modern Art, New York. Mrs. Stanley Resor Fund (by exchange). *See plates 35–37.* Artists: André Beaudin, Camille Bryen, André Derain, Max Ernst, Alberto Giacometti, Alberto Magnelli, Louis Marcoussis, André Masson, Joan Miró, Jules Pascin, Picasso, André Dunoyer de Segonzac, Léopold Survage. Preparatory mate-

rial: Ernst, three annotated states of etching, hand-colored *bon à tirer* of etching corrected by Ernst, photocopies of same annotated by Iliazd; Magnelli, four proofs of etching with aquatint; Picasso, unique proof of Picasso's handwritten engraving of his text, *bon à tirer* of Iliazd's typographical version of same, signed by Picasso ††. Iliazd, chart directing placement of artists' signatures †.

Villon, Jacques   **French, 1875–1963**

34. *Ajournement* by André du Bouchet. Paris, À l'éditeur qui ne fait pas aciérer les planches de cuivre (Iliazd), 1960. Seven etchings executed by Marcel Fiorini after drawings by Villon, 16½ × 5½–11¹⁄₁₆" (42 × 14–28.1 cm) (folded variable widths). The Museum of Modern Art, New York. Gift of Raymond J. Learsy. *See plate 30.*

Zdanevitch, Kiril   **Russian, 1892–1969**

35. *Rekord niezhnosti* ("Record of Tenderness") by Igor Terentiev. Tiflis, 41°, 1919. Ten linoleum cuts, printed in color, 6⅛ × 5½" (15.5 × 14 cm). Private collection. *See plate 3.*

DRAWINGS, POSTERS, AND ANNOUNCEMENTS
Sheet dimensions are given in inches and centimeters, height preceding width.

Delaunay, Robert   **French, 1885–1941**

36. *Portrait of Iliazd*. 1922. Crayon, 17⅛ × 12⅛" (43.5 × 30.7 cm). The Museum of Modern Art, New York. Purchase.

Gontcharova, Natalia

37. *Portrait of Ilia Zdanevitch*. 1913. Pen and ink, 14³⁄₁₆ × 10¼" (36 × 26 cm). Private collection.

Iliazd (Ilia Zdanevitch)

38. Poster for Futurist conference at Borjoum, Georgia. c. 1917–18. Lithograph, 42⅛ × 27⁹⁄₁₆" (107 × 70 cm). Private collection.
39. Poster for conference "L'Eloge d'Ilia Zdanevitch surnommé l'ange," May 12, 1922. Lithograph, 21⅜ × 19⅛" (54.3 × 48.7 cm). The Museum of Modern Art, New York. Arthur A. Cohen Purchase Fund.
40. Announcement for conference given by Iliazd, Tristan Tzara, Paul Eluard, and Philippe Soupault, November 28, 1922. Watercolor, 10⅝ × 8¼" (27 × 21 cm). Private collection.
41. Souvenir program for "Bal transmental," February 23, 1923. Collage, 6⅞" (17.6 cm) diameter. Private collection.
42. Poster/program for "La Soirée du *Coeur à barbe*," July 6, 1923. 16⅛ × 10¼" (41 × 26 cm). Private collection.

Iliazd and
André Lhote   French, 1885–1962

43. Poster for costume ball "Fête de nuit à Montparnasse,"
June 20, 1922. Lithograph, 55⅛ × 36" (140 × 91.5 cm).
Private collection.

Miró, Joan

44. *Portrait of Iliazd.* 1968. Gouache, 14⁹⁄₁₆ × 11⅝" (55 × 37 cm).
Private collection.

Waliszewski, Zygmunt   Polish, 1897–1936

45. Untitled caricature of Iliazd addressing donkeys. 1919. Pen and
ink, 7½ × 9¼" (19 × 23.5 cm). Private collection.

PHOTOGRAPH CREDITS

The photographers and sources of the illustrations in this book are listed alphabetically below, followed by the number of the page on which each illustration appears.

Michel Auder: 2; Jean Dubout, Paris: 40, 41, 59 left, 62, 64, 65; Jacques Faujour, Paris: 55 top, 56 left, 57, 60, 61, 68, 71; Archives Iliazd, Paris: 23, 26, 53 bottom right, 54 right, 55 bottom left, 76, 78, 79, 80; Luc Joubert, Paris: 33, 53 top right, 54 left; Kate Keller, The Museum of Modern Art: 10 right, 13, 15, 22, 67 bottom; Patrice Lefebvre, Galerie d'art de L'Université du Québec à Montréal: 63, 66 right; Mali Olatunji, The Museum of Modern Art: 40, 55 bottom right, 56 right, 58, 59 center and right, 66 left, 67 top, 70, 72, 73, 74, 75; Robert D. Rubic, New York: 53 left, 69; Soichi Sunami, The Museum of Modern Art: 14.

TRUSTEES OF

THE MUSEUM OF MODERN ART

William S. Paley, *Chairman Emeritus*
Mrs. John D. Rockefeller 3rd, *Chairman of the Board*
Mrs. Henry Ives Cobb, *Vice Chairman*
David Rockefeller, *Vice Chairman*
Donald B. Marron, *President*
Mrs. Frank Y. Larkin, *Vice President*
John Parkinson III, *Vice President and Treasurer*

Lily Auchincloss
Edward Larrabee Barnes
Celeste G. Bartos
Sid Richardson Bass
H.R.H. Prinz Franz von Bayern**
Gordon Bunshaft
Shirley C. Burden
Thomas S. Carroll*
John B. Carter
Gianluigi Gabetti
Miss Lillian Gish**
Paul Gottlieb
Agnes Gund
Mrs. Melville Wakeman Hall
George Heard Hamilton*
Barbara Jakobson
Sidney Janis**
Philip Johnson
Ronald S. Lauder
John L. Loeb*
Ranald H. Macdonald*
David H. McAlpin**
Dorothy C. Miller**
J. Irwin Miller*
S. I. Newhouse, Jr.
Philip S. Niarchos

Richard E. Oldenburg
Peter G. Peterson
Gifford Phillips
John Rewald**
David Rockefeller, Jr.
Richard E. Salomon
Mrs. Wolfgang Schoenborn*
Mrs. Constantine Sidamon-Eristoff
Mrs. Bertram Smith
Jerry I. Speyer
Mrs. Alfred R. Stern
Mrs. Donald B. Straus
Walter N. Thayer
R. L. B. Tobin
Monroe Wheeler*
Richard S. Zeisler

Trustee Emeritus
**Honorary Trustee*

Ex Officio Trustees
Edward I. Koch, *Mayor of the City of New York*
Harrison J. Goldin, *Comptroller of the City of New York*
Joann K. Phillips, *President of The International Council*